New First Certificate
Masterclass

Video Activity Book

for the development of writing skills

Simon Haines
Barbara Stewart

Oxford University Press

Oxford University Press
Great Clarendon Street, Oxford OX2 6DP

Oxford   New York
Athens   Auckland   Bangkok   Bogotá   Buenos Aires
Calcutta   Cape Town   Chennai   Dar es Salaam
Delhi   Florence   Hong Kong   Istanbul   Karachi
Kuala Lumpur   Madrid   Melbourne   Mexico City
Mumbai   Nairobi   Paris   São Paulo   Singapore
Taipei   Tokyo   Toronto   Warsaw

and associated companies in
Berlin   Ibadan

OXFORD and OXFORD ENGLISH are
trade marks of Oxford University Press

First published 1997
Third impression 1999

ISBN 019 459001 1 (Activity Book)
ISBN 019 459002 X (Video Guide)

ISBN 019 458997 8 (VHS PAL Video Cassette 1)
ISBN 019 458998 6 (VHS SECAM Video Cassette 1)
ISBN 019 458999 4 (VHS NTSC Video Cassette 1)

ISBN 019 459008 9 (VHS PAL Video Cassette 2)
ISBN 019 459009 7 (VHS SECAM Video Cassette 2)
ISBN 019 459010 0 (VHS NTSC Video Cassette 2)

ISBN 019 459012 7 (VHS PAL Video Double Pack)
ISBN 019 459013 5 (VHS SECAM Video Double Pack)
ISBN 019 459014 3 (VHS NTSC Video Double Pack)

© Oxford University Press, 1997

No unauthorized photocopying

All rights reserved. No part of this publication may be reproduced, stored in a retrieval system, or transmitted, in any form or by any means, electronic, mechanical, photocopying, recording, or otherwise, without the prior written permission of Oxford University Press.

This book is sold subject to the condition that it shall not, by way of trade or otherwise, be lent, resold, hired out, or otherwise circulated without the publisher's prior consent in any form of binding or cover other than that in which it is published and without a similar condition including this condition being imposed on the subsequent purchaser.

Printed in Hong Kong

Stills photography
Rob Judges
Rob Cousins

Acknowledgements
The publisher would like to thank the following for permission to reproduce photographs:

Acquarius, page 36 (Lion King poster, ET poster, Jurassic Park poster, Star Wars poster)

Corbis/ Nik Wheeler, page 49 (Mijas street scene)

Kobal Collection, page 36 (Ghost poster)

Tony Stone/Mark Wagner, page 49 (open road)

Sygma, page 35, G. Arci (Robert de Niro), E. Robert (Kevin Kostner), R. Simoneit (Emma Thompson), Frank Trapper (Jim Carrey)

Travel Ink/David Toase, page 49 (people and cars)

Extra Commissioned photography by:

Rob Judges, page 44 (tourist guide)

Mark Mason, page 17 (chocolate), page 22 (foods)

CONTENTS

INTRODUCTION   4

WRITING IN THE FIRST CERTIFICATE EXAMINATION   5

All You Need to Know
WRITING A TRANSACTIONAL LETTER   6

The Temptation of Chocolate
WRITING AN ARTICLE   15

A Case of Mistaken Identity
WRITING A STORY   24

The Silver Screen
WRITING A REPORT   32

Yours Faithfully
WRITING A LETTER OF APPLICATION   41

The Dream Machine
WRITING A DISCURSIVE COMPOSITION   49

SAMPLE QUESTIONS AND ANSWERS   58

WRITING BANK   64

INTRODUCTION

About this video Activity Book

This Activity Book and the video it accompanies have been produced to help you to improve your writing skills and to give you a better chance of passing the Writing paper of the First Certificate examination.

The video and the book are divided into six units, each of which focuses in detail on one of the task types in Paper 2. We hope that by working through these units you will develop good general writing habits as well as preparing yourself for the examination.

The six units are in no particular order, but we have started with the Transactional letter because this is the one question everyone has to answer.

Each unit starts with a brief introduction and then has four main sections.

Introduction
This gives a description and one or two examples of the task type which is the focus of the unit.

Think ahead
This section prepares you for watching the video by introducing the topic or subject matter of the video. For example, the topic of unit one is 'Your Ideal Language School'.

In 'Think ahead' sections you may be asked to complete a questionnaire or discuss questions with other students.

Viewing
The video units range between 5 and 9 minutes in length. Sometimes you will be asked to watch the video without stopping; sometimes you will watch section by section.

You will always have 'before you watch' and 'while you watch' tasks to complete. Usually this section provides you with information and ideas which you can incorporate in your own writing later in the unit.

Preparation for writing
These sections vary from unit to unit but most include notes on structure (paragraphing, layout, etc.), style, vocabulary, grammar, and connecting ideas. There are guidelines, examples and practice activities to help you in these specific areas.

Writing
This final section includes an examination question related to the topic of the video as well as extra practice questions. There are also Guidelines which summarize the main points to be considered when doing each particular writing task type.

A reference section at the back of the book includes:

Sample questions and answers for each task type
The sample answers include notes pointing out and summarizing the key features of each task type. They are not the answers to the questions set in the 'Writing' sections of the Activity Book. (The Video Guide for teachers contains sample answers to these questions.)

Writing bank
This lists useful connecting words and phrases as well as notes on formal and informal writing styles.

The video

The two twenty-six minute video cassettes present six units or programmes – three dramas and three documentaries. Used with the Activity Book, the main purpose of the videos is to provide you with ideas to write about, but of course we hope that you will also find the programmes informative, interesting and perhaps amusing.

WRITING IN THE FIRST CERTIFICATE EXAMINATION

The Writing paper

The Writing paper of the First Certificate in English (FCE) examination, Paper 2, lasts 1 hour 30 minutes and has two parts.

Part 1 is compulsory – it must be answered by all candidates.

Part 2 includes four questions from which candidates must answer one.

Summary of Paper 2		
Task type and focus	Number of tasks and length	Task format
Part 1, Question 1 Transactional letter.	One compulsory task of 120-180 words.	Candidates answer a letter related to a situation outlined in one or more short texts, rubric* and sometimes visuals.
Part 2, Questions 2 - 4 Article, Report, Informal letter (non-transactional), Letter of application, Composition, Story.	Choice of three tasks, each of 120-180 words.	Candidates do 'real-life', situational writing tasks presented through rubric*.
Question 5 Composition, article, report or letter on a prescribed reading text.	Choice of two tasks, each of 120-180 words.	Candidates do a task presented through rubric*.

* A *rubric* describes or explains what students should do.

What is important in the Writing paper?

In all your writing tasks you should try to use correct grammar, appropriate vocabulary, and punctuate and spell correctly. Of course, you shouldn't write less than 120 words or much more than 180 words for each answer. However, to pass the First Certificate examination you also need to do the following:

- **Read the question carefully and answer all parts of it**
  Some candidates get a low mark simply because they do not answer the question or they fail to notice an important part of the question. It is particularly important in **Question 1** that you read ALL the information you are given and think carefully about what is required.

- **Distinguish between task types**
  The question will tell you whether you should write an **article**, a **report**, or a **composition**, etc. Think carefully about the characteristics of the task type before you start to write.

- **Think about the purpose of the piece of writing**
  Your writing will be marked partly on how well it serves its purpose. For example, in your answer to Question 1, the examiner will assess how effective your transactional letter would be in a real-life situation. This means writing in an appropriate style and making it very clear to the person you are writing to exactly what response you expect him or her to make.

- **Think about who you are writing to or for**
  The *target reader* is of great importance. For example, you may be asked to write an article for 'young people' in your country. Before you start writing, think carefully about these people, their situation and the kind of writing they would find interesting.

- **Decide on an appropriate style**
  The task type, the purpose of a piece of writing and the target reader, are all factors to take into account when you decide what style to write in. For most examination tasks, there are two basic choices: *formal* or *informal*. Familiarize yourself with the features of these kinds of writing and use the style which is best suited to the task. For example, the transactional letter can be formal or informal, but the non-transactional letter in Part 2 is always informal, and the letter of application in Part 2 is always formal.

- **Decide on the correct layout**
  Sometimes you may need to think about the layout of your writing. For example, if you write a report, it would be sensible to think about dividing your writing into sections with headings which indicate the content of that section.

Taken together, these points suggest that a sensible approach to dealing with each question you answer in Paper 2 would be as follows:

1 **Read** the question carefully, at least twice.
2 **Think** about the purpose of the writing and who you are writing to or for.
3 **Decide** on a style which is appropriate to the task type.
4 **Plan** your answers before you start writing. This can be on paper or in your head. Think about how many paragraphs or sections your writing should have, and whether you should incorporate any special layout features.
5 **Start** writing.

And don't forget: allow yourself time – 5 minutes for each question if possible – to read through and correct what you have written!

WRITING A TRANSACTIONAL LETTER Paper 2, Part 1

All You Need to Know

The first question in the Writing paper of the First Certificate in English (FCE) examination, which all candidates have to answer, is a **transactional letter**. This type of letter can initiate action, such as a letter of invitation, or be a response to a request for action, for example a reply to a newspaper advertisement. You may be required to write in an informal or a formal style. More examples of transactional letters include: booking a holiday, making a complaint, requesting information.

Think ahead

Your ideal language school

1 If you were planning to study English in Britain, what kind of school would you choose? Make notes under the headings at the top of page 7.

How long does it take to ...?
How long it takes to

- **The location**
  near to the downtown

- **In the classroom**

- **Out of class activities**
  classes of music and theatre

- **Accommodation**
  house of family

- **Other things that are important to you personally**

2 Now compare your notes with a partner's.

Your reply to the advert

Study in Oxford
at

The Bolingbroke School of English

Centre of Excellence since 1967

- General English courses
- Examination preparation
- Business English
- Short summer courses

Send for our free video showing life at the school

Write to:
The Principal,
The Bolingbroke School of English,

In response to an advertisement in a magazine, you sent away for a promotional video about The Bolingbroke School of English in Oxford.

What information about life at the school would you expect the video to tell you?

Write a list of questions in the left-hand column. The first one has been done as an example.

Questions:	Answers:
How many students are there at the school?	
How many students are there at the bedroom	There are two students in the bedroom
What can I do in my free time?	you can go to visit museums
Can I travel in the weekends	it depends

WRITING A TRANSACTIONAL LETTER   7

Viewing

First viewing

Watch *All you need to know* from beginning to end and answer these questions.

1 How well does the school compare with the ideal language school you described in **Think ahead**, Your ideal language school, on page 7? Tick (✓) any of your ideal features which are shown in the video.

2 Does the video answer any of the questions you wrote in **Think ahead**, Your reply to the advert, on page 7? Note down the answers in the right-hand column.

Initial reactions

1 What do you think about The Bolingbroke School? Would you like to study there? Why? Why not?

Make lists of the attractive and less attractive features.

Attractive features	Less attractive features

2 Discuss your ideas in small groups.

WRITING A TRANSACTIONAL LETTER

The video about The Bolingbroke School contains a lot of general information but leaves out details that you may want to know.

Watch the video again and make a note of anything you would like more information about.

Section 1
0.00 – 1.06

Opening sequence

Where is the city?
How far is from the centre?
Tourists place to visit

Section 2
1.08 – 2.32

THE IDEAL WAY TO LEARN

What kind of course?
of technology
How many students in the class?

Section 3
2.34 – 3.20

OUTSIDE THE CLASSROOM

What are the facilities about sport?
Where are they taking you to visit?
Price for the activity?

Section 4
3.22 – 4.56

WHERE TO STAY
(Including eating arrangements)

How far are the homes from the school?
How many students stays on the same bedroom on the school?
How reasonable are the prices for food?

WRITING A TRANSACTIONAL LETTER

Preparing for writing

Asking for specific information

Here are some of the general statements and vague expressions used in the promotional video for the school.

1 For each statement write a question asking for more precise information.

Statement:	Question:
... the school is within easy reach of the city centre ...	(Exactly) How far is the school from the city centre?
a ... many places of historical and cultural interest.	
b We provide an extensive choice of courses ...	
c ... and cater for a wide age range.	
d ... (class) numbers are kept to an absolute minimum.	
e The school has excellent facilities ...	
f The most up-to-date methods and technology are used ...	
g ... there is a full range of sporting facilities.	
h There is also a varied programme of social and leisure activities.	
i ... visiting places of interest ...	
j ... we can make other (accommodation) arrangements for you.	
k ... a wide variety of hot meals, snacks and refreshments ...	
l ... at very reasonable prices.	

2 If you were thinking of studying at The Bolingbroke School, which three or four questions would you most want answers to?

3 Compare your ideas with a partner's.

WRITING A TRANSACTIONAL LETTER

Style

Depending on the context, transactional letters may be written in an informal or a formal style.

1 Look at these sets of expressions and decide which would be the most appropriate expression in a letter asking for more information about The Bolingbroke School of English. Circle the correct number.

a 1 Dear John
   2 Dear Sir or Madam
   3 Dear Principal

b 1 Thank you for sending me your school video.
   2 Thanks for the video, I thought it was brilliant.
   3 I really liked your video – thanks.

c 1 You don't say exactly how far the school is from the middle of Oxford.
   2 I was wondering exactly how far it is from the school to Oxford city centre.
   3 How long do you reckon it'd take to walk to the town centre?

d 1 Perhaps you could let me know what the average class size is?
   2 I want to know how many students there are in a class.
   3 Might I enquire about the maximum number of students allowed in each class?

e 1 What do most students do after classes?
   2 How do your students spend their free time? I mean, is there a lot to do in Oxford?
   3 I would be grateful if you could send me a detailed social programme for a typical week at the school.

f 1 Please send me the details I have requested as soon as possible.
   2 Get the information to me as soon as you can, please.
   3 I would be eternally grateful if you could manage to send me the information detailed above at your earliest convenience.

g 1 Can't wait to hear from you.
   2 I look forward to hearing from you.
   3 I shall expect to hear from you by the end of this week.

2 Compare your ideas with a partner's. Decide together what is wrong with the two expressions you have rejected in each case.

Structure

As well as writing in an appropriate style, you should also take care to structure your letter carefully. This means grouping information and ideas systematically, and starting a new paragraph each time the topic focus changes.

Discuss these questions with a partner. First discuss the questions generally, and then discuss them with reference to a letter to The Bolingbroke School asking for further information.

1 What should you write in the first paragraph of a transactional letter?

2 What should you write in the second and subsequent paragraphs?

3 What is the purpose of the last paragraph of a transactional letter? (Remember that some letters like this expect an outcome or a result.)

4 How should you end a letter which starts *Dear Sir or Madam,* ?

WRITING A TRANSACTIONAL LETTER

Connecting ideas

In all kinds of writing, it is important to structure what we write by incorporating words or phrases which help the reader to understand the organization of the text. These include:

- words or phrases which introduce additional information

    *My favourite sports are tennis and squash, but **in addition** to these I also like swimming and riding.*

    in addition (to these) ...

- words or phrases which introduce contrasting information

    *I don't particularly like busy cities. **On the other hand**, I don't want to live in the middle of the country.*

    on the other hand ...

- words or phrases which summarize or conclude

    *I've got no money, so I can't go anywhere. I've got lots of free time, but nothing to do. **In short**, I need a job.*

    in short ...

- words or phrases which list

    *There are a number of questions I'd like to ask. **First of all**, how many lessons are there a day?*

    first of all ...

- words or phrases which introduce an example

    *I'd like to know about any additional expenses, **for instance**, how much is the bus fare into town?*

    for instance ...

Add more words and phrases to the five categories above.

WRITING A TRANSACTIONAL LETTER

Vocabulary

Compound nouns

In English it is common to use two nouns together instead of a longer phrase. Using compound nouns is a natural and economical use of words. For example, it is usually better to use *window cleaner* than *a man who cleans windows*, and *city centre* is more natural than *the centre of the city*. The first noun in each pair is often singular.

1 Underline the compound nouns in these extracts from the video script.

   a ... we have a growing international reputation for the excellence of our teachers and our teaching methods.

   b ... and cater for a wide age range.

   c ... class size is considered to be particularly important ...

   d The most up-to-date methods and technology are used to help you develop your language skills.

   e There is also a varied programme of social and leisure activities.

2 What compound nouns could be used instead of the underlined phrases in these sentences?

   a The <u>principal of the college</u> welcomes all students personally.

   ....

   b <u>Numbers of students</u> are increasing year by year.

   all
   ....

   c Most of the <u>buildings of the school</u> are over a hundred years old.

   ....

   d The school has weekly <u>classes which prepare students for exams</u>. (3 - noun compound)

   ....

   e The school has a busy programme of <u>activities in the afternoons</u>.

   ....

   f We have recently installed a <u>laboratory to help students to learn languages</u>.

   ....

3 Make compound nouns by matching a word in list **A** with a word in list **B**. Often more than one combination is possible. Think about whether the compound nouns are written as one word (e.g. *bookshop*), as two words (e.g. *railway station*) or whether they are joined by a hyphen (e.g. *bus-driver*).

A	B
a school	court
b meal	trip
c day	activity
d leisure	room
e student	time
f class	building
g tennis	programme
h weekend	discount

Check your compound nouns in a dictionary. How are they written?

WRITING A TRANSACTIONAL LETTER

Writing

You have just finished watching the video about The Bolingbroke School of English. You are disappointed that the video did not provide you with all the information you were expecting.

Write a **letter** of between **120 and 180** words in an appropriate style asking for more detailed information. Do not include addresses.

Refer to the notes you wrote in **Viewing**, Sections 1-4, on page 9, the questions you wrote in **Preparing for writing** on page 10 and the ideas you had about composition structure in **Preparing for writing**, Structure, on page 11.

Work through the **Guidelines** below before you start writing.

Extra practice

In the Writing paper of the FCE examination the information you are given is **written** rather than in the form of a video recording. Here is another sample Part 1 question.

You are looking for a different kind of holiday, and you find an interesting advertisement in a magazine. You like the idea of an *active interest holiday*, but you would like some more information. You have made a few rough notes on the advertisement.

Read carefully the advertisement and the notes which you have made. Then write a letter to the holiday company, covering the points in your notes and adding any relevant information about yourself.

- Bored with beaches?
- Sick of sightseeing?
- Tired of other tourists?

Then why not have a change and try one of our Active Interest Holidays?

We offer a wide range of activity holidays to suit all tastes. Most of our centres are located in some of Europe's beautiful cities.

We make all the necessary arrangements but we offer you a choice of means of travel and type of accommodation.

For further information, please write to:

Active Interest Holidays,
7 Bishopsgate,
West Torham. PP2 6QA

Handwritten notes: Is there a complete list? / Which cities? / What choices? Flying? / What kinds? Camping? / Prices?

Write a **letter** of between **120 and 180** words in an appropriate style. Do not write any addresses.

Guidelines

✓ Do

- Read the information provided in the question.
- Decide how you are going to use all this information in your letter.
- Plan your letter carefully. Work out a paragraph plan, deciding on the number of paragraphs and the topic and purpose of each paragraph. Think particularly carefully about appropriate first and last sentences for your letter.
- Think about who you are writing to, and decide on the appropriate style to use. How will your letter start and end?
- Write your letter, following your plan and including all the information.
- Check grammar, style, spelling and punctuation.

✗ Don't

- Don't start writing until you have read and understood the information in the question.
- Don't forget that in your answer you have to cover all the essential points included in the question.
- Don't write anything until you have a clear idea of the structure of your letter and the content of each of the paragraphs.
- Don't use contractions or other informal language unless you are writing to a friend.

WRITING A TRANSACTIONAL LETTER

WRITING AN ARTICLE Paper 2, Part 2

The Temptation of Chocolate

In Part 2 of the Writing paper of the First Certificate in English (FCE) examination, one of the choices may be to write an **article**. The examination question will tell you what the topic of the article is, where it will be published (e.g. *a magazine*), and who you are writing it for.

Articles can be lighthearted or more serious in style and usually contain a mixture of information and opinion. You can give your own opinion on the topic or write in a more impersonal way.

Example:

You see this announcement in a magazine for young people.

Write a short **article** for this magazine giving your ideas.

WORLD TEENAGER MAGAZINE $2 — What do you think? Are we eating the wrong sorts of food? Write us your answer to this question based on your own experience.

Think ahead

Introduction

Discuss these questions with a partner.

1 What is chocolate made from?

2 Which countries are famous for making chocolate? In your opinion, which country makes the best chocolate?

3 Can you explain the difference between the following?

> chocolate   a chocolate   a bar of chocolate
> a piece of chocolate   a box of chocolates

Questionnaire

Ask a partner these questions and note down their answers. Add two questions of your own.

1	Do you eat chocolate?	☐ Yes ☐ No
2	How many bars of chocolate do you eat a week?	☐
3	Do you think you eat too much chocolate?	☐ Yes ☐ No
4	Do you eat one particular brand of chocolate?	☐ Yes ☐ No
	If 'Yes', which?	
5	When do you usually eat chocolate?	☐ at meals ☐ between meals
6	Do you ever give chocolate as a present?	☐ Yes ☐ No
	If 'Yes', When do you give it?	
	Who do you give it to?	
	Why do you give it?	
7	Are you ever given chocolate as a present?	☐ Yes ☐ No
	If 'Yes', Do you like being given it?	☐
	Would you prefer something else?	☐
8	?	
9	?	

Discussion

Discuss these questions.

1 Why do you think so many people eat chocolate?

2 Do you think chocolate is good for you or bad for you? Give reasons.

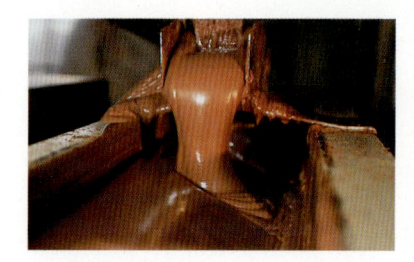

WRITING AN ARTICLE

Viewing

Section 1
0.00 - 1.52

Before you watch

The first section of the video you are going to see introduces the topic of chocolate. Before you watch, discuss these questions.

1 Which of the countries listed below do you think are the top three consumers of chocolate?

Swich

austria

Norway

2 Which country do you think consumes the least chocolate?

....

3 Where would you place your country in the list?

....

Argentina	Germany	Norway
Austria	Great Britain	Poland
Belgium	Italy	Spain
Brazil	Japan	Switzerland
France	Luxembourg	USA

4 In Britain, who do you think eats more chocolate, children or young adults?

While you watch

Watch this section and check your ideas to **Before you watch**. Do you think the answer to question 4 would be the same for your country?

Section 2
1.53 - 2.20

Before you watch

In this section of the video you will see a commercial for a bar of chocolate.

1 Think of some TV commercials for chocolate in your country. Describe your favourite and say why you like it.

2 You are going to see a commercial for Cadbury's flake. In the commercial a young woman carrying some sheets of music and a cello, is walking across a famous bridge in Prague. Predict the answers to these questions.

  a What happens in the commercial? *She going to meet a man*

  b How does the woman eat the chocolate?

  c What kind of background music is played?

While you watch

Watch this section of the video. How different were your ideas?

WRITING AN ARTICLE

(+) savoury ≠ salty (-)

Section 3
2.21 - 4.53

Before you watch

In this section of the video, the presenter interviews Caroline Sarll, the founder of a society called *Chocoholics Unanimous*.

1 Predict two activities that the society organizes for its members.

dedicate to chocolate

about 6 meets a year

2 Look at the pictures below of the food they eat during their meal. Try to describe the dishes. Then, make a list of any adjectives or phrases you think the presenter or Caroline Sarll will use to describe how the food tastes.

That's gorgeous! delicious, wonderful, luxury

While you watch

1 Watch this section and check your ideas to **Before you watch 1** and **2**.

2 Watch the section again and make a note below of any different adjectives and phrases you heard.

WRITING AN ARTICLE

well be ... gorgeous

Section 4

4.54 – 6.40

Before you watch

In this section you are going to hear part of an interview with a dietician. Before you watch, decide if these sentences are true (**T**) or false (**F**). Mark the boxes.

a Chocolate is low in fat but high in sugar. ☐ F

b Chocolate is bad for our health. ☐

c Chocolate is addictive. ☐ T

d Carbohydrates like pasta, bread, rice and cereals give us more energy than chocolate. ☐ T

e Chocolate contains important vitamins and minerals. ☐ F

f It is reasonable to eat one bar of chocolate a day providing the rest of one's diet is balanced. ☐ F

guilt dedicate to us

While you watch

Watch this section. Check your answers. Correct any false information.

Section 5

6.41 – 9.05

Before you watch

In this section you are going to hear the presenter talking about the history of chocolate before speaking to George Dadd, who checks the quality of the chocolate at Cadbury's factory in Birmingham.

1 Answer this quick quiz.

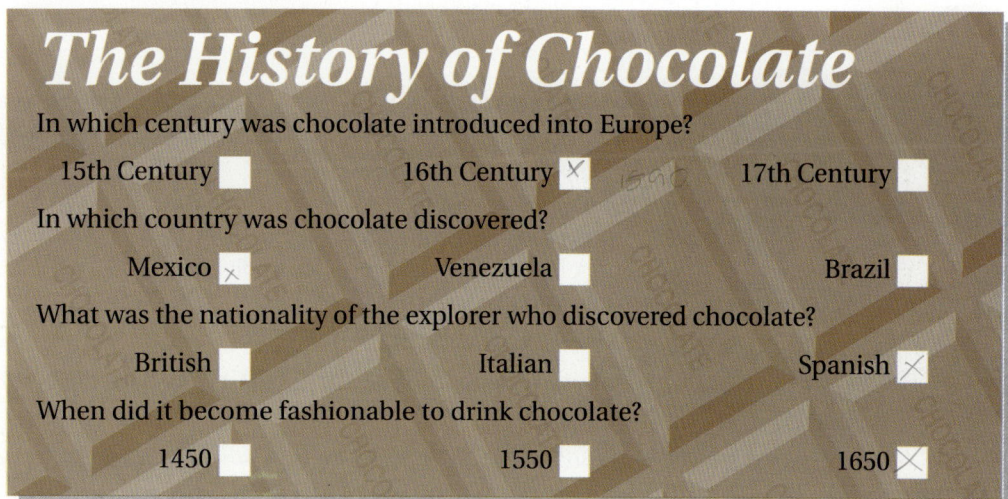

The History of Chocolate

In which century was chocolate introduced into Europe?

   15th Century ☐   16th Century ☒   17th Century ☐

In which country was chocolate discovered?

   Mexico ☒   Venezuela ☐   Brazil ☐

What was the nationality of the explorer who discovered chocolate?

   British ☐   Italian ☐   Spanish ☒

When did it become fashionable to drink chocolate?

   1450 ☐   1550 ☐   1650 ☒

2 Predict the questions the presenter asks George Dadd about chocolate and his job.

....

....

While you watch *he is tasted chocolate*

1 Watch this section and check your answers to **Before you watch 1** and **2**.

2 Watch the section with George Dadd again. Write down the first question he is asked and his answer to it.

Q: ....

A: ....

WRITING AN ARTICLE 19

Preparing for writing

Structure

Articles frequently follow this pattern:

> **Title**
> This should attract the reader's interest and give some idea of what the article is about. It should be appropriate to the style of the article.
>
> **First paragraph**
> The opening sentence is especially important. It should:
> - introduce the topic;
> - make a link between the title and the first paragraph;
> - make the reader want to continue reading.
>
> The remainder of the first paragraph should develop the topic and maintain the reader's interest.
>
> **Middle paragraphs**
> The middle paragraphs should continue to develop the topic.
>
> **Final paragraph**
> This should round off the article.

1 Title

1 Read these article titles. Which would make you want to read the article? Which wouldn't? Give reasons.

  a Chocolate
  b My idea of heaven
  c Confessions of a chocoholic
  d Chocolate: Society's acceptable addiction
  e Could you live without it?
  f Looking after your health: Chocolate

2 Which titles are appropriate for a light-hearted article? Which are appropriate for a more serious article? Which are appropriate for both?

2 First paragraph

1 Read through these titles and first paragraphs. One is taken from a magazine article, the others were written by students of English. How effective are they?

> **A** *Chocolate*
> I eat at least two bars of chocolate a day and in my view that's O.K. It's better for you than cigarettes anyway - well, you don't get lung cancer from eating chocolate. And you have to have one vice, don't you?

> **B** *Chocolate: Society's acceptable addiction*
> Many people find chocolate hard to resist, but is it actually addictive? Research seems to suggest that it is not possible to become physically addicted to chocolate in the same way as to substances such as nicotine in tobacco.

> **C** *Could you live without it?*
> Some people say they could but wouldn't want to. Others say that they've tried but that it's impossible. What are we talking about? Chocolate!

WRITING AN ARTICLE

PROS & CONS

D *My idea of heaven*
There is nothing nicer on a cold winter's evening than relaxing in a nice, hot bath listening to music and eating a bar of chocolate. And it seems that I'm not the only one who puts it top of their list of pleasures.

2 Which paragraph(s) B, C or D is written in a light-hearted style and which in a more serious style? Pick out some features of each style and list them.

....

....

3 These techniques are commonly used to introduce a topic. Match them to the paragraphs above. More than one technique may be used in the same paragraph.

a Ask a question.
b Give a strong opinion.
c Describe a problem which requires an answer.
d Describe an interesting scene or situation.

3 Middle paragraphs (*extracts*)

1 Match these middle paragraph extracts with their first paragraphs above.

You've heard of 'alcoholics' and 'workaholics'. Now there are also 'chocoholics'. Believe it or not, they even have their own society, 'Chocoholics Unanimous'. ☐

However, not everyone agrees. Ms. Corinne Sweet, a counsellor with the Eating Disorders Association, believes that people can become addicted to chocolate. ☐

Apparently, the time of year doesn't make any difference. We eat as much in the summer as we do in the winter. Did you know that the average British person eats an incredible 7.3 kilograms a year? The Swiss get through even more! ☐

Some of my friends don't eat meals, just chocolate and crisps and things like that. I don't think that's a good idea. It's bad for your health. You should have a balanced diet. ☐

2 How did you decide which middle paragraphs went with each first paragraph? How effective are the middle paragraphs?

4 Final paragraph

The final paragraph should round off the article in some way. Writers often do this by using one or more of the following techniques. Match these techniques with the final paragraphs below.

a Summarizing the main points of the article.
b Expressing a final personal opinion on the theme of the article.
c Leaving the reader with something to think about (or a question to answer).

A I think it's O.K. to eat chocolate, but you should eat a balanced diet, too. ☐

B It would seem then that, though chocolate does not appear to be physically addictive, there are indications that it may be emotionally and psychologically addictive. It is not referred to as 'comfort food' for nothing! ☐

C Be honest with yourself. Could you give it up? ☐

D Whether eaten or drunk, chocolate just has to be one of the best things in life. ☐

WRITING AN ARTICLE 21

Connecting ideas

Referring words such as personal pronouns (e.g. *it*), demonstrative pronouns (e.g *this*) and relative pronouns (e.g. *which*) help to link a text together and improve it by avoiding the repetition of single words and clauses.

1 Underline the referring words in this extract from the video and say what they refer to.

Chocoholics Unanimous is a chocolate appreciation society, which I set up in 1990. It is a society dedicated to the consumption and the enjoyment of chocolate in all its shapes and forms. We meet about five or six times a year.

2 Fill the gaps in these extracts from the video and the magazine article on chocolate with an appropriate referring word.

a The problem with a diet .... is very high in fat and sugar is that .... is linked to heart disease.

b When Hernan Cortes conquered Mexico in 1519, ... discovered that the Aztecs had been drinking chocolate for hundreds of years. On .... return to Spain, Cortes took with .... cocoa beans and equipment for making chocolate. .... remained a Spanish secret for almost one hundred years before Cortes' discovery spread to other European countries.

c The reason why we crave chocolate lies in .... chemical composition: .... contains over three hundred chemicals. .... give chocolate .... distinctive flavour and texture.

d Can you imagine eating 7.3 kilograms of chocolate? .... is how much the average person in Britain gets through each year. .... is equivalent to eating eighteen of these giant bars of milk chocolate.

Vocabulary

1 The following adjectives can all be used to describe chocolate. Do they describe its taste, its texture or both? Use a dictionary if necessary.

sweet   bitter   creamy   smooth   crunchy

2 Match the adjectives below with the food and drink in the pictures. Then describe something you have eaten or drunk recently using as many descriptive adjectives as you can.

bitter   creamy   crispy   crunchy   salty   sickly   sour

WRITING AN ARTICLE

Writing

Write an **article** of between **120 and 180** words in answer to the examination question on page 15. Use any ideas that you have noted down from the video and any ideas of your own.

Work through the **Guidelines** below before you start writing.

Extra practice

Write another **article** of between **120 and 180** words for the same magazine in answer to this question.

> Do young people today take enough exercise?

Guidelines

✓ Do

- Read the question carefully so that you know exactly what you have to do.
- Decide whether you are going to write a light-hearted or a more serious article.
- Think of a good title. Remember that it should attract the reader and give some idea of the topic.
- Make some notes for each paragraph.
  First paragraph: This should relate to the title, be interesting, and make the reader want to continue reading.
  Middle paragraphs: These should develop your ideas.
  Final paragraph: This should round off the article.
- Expand your notes into complete sentences. Use appropriate words and phrases to connect your ideas and write in an appropriate style.
- Check grammar, style, spelling and punctuation.

✗ Don't

- Don't start writing immediately. The thinking and planning stages are important.
- Don't forget who you are writing for. One style may be more appropriate than another.
- Don't forget to think up a good title. It will help you to get a better mark.
- Don't only include information; include opinions as well.
- Don't mix styles. Write in informal English for a light-hearted article and in more formal English for a serious one.

WRITING A STORY Paper 2, Part 2

A Case of Mistaken Identity

In Part 2 of the Writing paper of the First Certificate in English (FCE) examination, one of the choices may be to write a **story**. A story is a piece of imaginative writing with a beginning, a middle and an end. It gives an account of real or imagined events.

The exam question will give you the first or last sentence of the story. You will be asked to complete the story in between **120 and 180** words.

Example:

> Your language school is running a short story competition. The competition rules say that the story must begin with the following words:
>
> *Michael's problems began as soon as he arrived at work that morning.*
>
> Write your **story** for the competition.

Think ahead

Discussion

1 What makes a good story? In groups, draw up a list of four or five factors you think are important.

2 Tell the other people in your group about a story you have read recently which you liked. Say what it was about and why you liked it.

Getting ideas

In the video which you are going to watch a student is planning her answer to this examination question.

> Write a **story** beginning with these words:
>
> *Jonathan left home at the usual time that morning.*

1 Write down the questions you would ask yourself and the possible answers.

   Example: Who is Jonathan? – A student? A businessman? A pilot?

   ....

   ....

2 Write down in 10-15 words what your story will be about. Don't write any details. Then compare ideas with a partner.

   ....

   ....

Viewing

Section 1
0.00 - 3.20

Before you watch

holder – possuidor

Before you watch the first section of the video, look at these photos and predict the story.

While you watch

Watch this section of the video and check your predictions.

WRITING A STORY   25

Section 2
3.21 - 6.17

Before you watch

In pairs tell the next part of the story. (**Note:** The photos are in the correct order.)

While you watch

Watch this section of the video and check your ideas.

Section 3
6.18 - 8.18

Before you watch

In pairs, predict what happens next. (**Note:** The woman in the shop is an important character!)

While you watch

1 Work in pairs:

Student A: Watch your section (6.18 - 7.06) without sound. Then tell your partner what you have seen. **Student B:** Sit with your back to the screen while your partner is watching. Then ask your partner questions to find out what happened.

Reverse roles. **Student B:** Watch your section (7.06 - 8.18) **without** sound and follow the same proceedure.

2 Watch the section with sound and picture. Were your ideas correct?

Section 4
8.19 - 9.05

Before you watch

In pairs, predict how the story ends. Use this photograph from the video to give you some ideas.

While you watch

Watch the final section and check your predictions. What do you think Jonathan will do now?

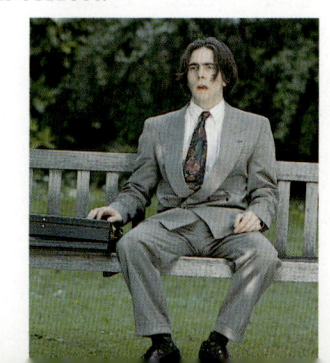

26 WRITING A STORY

Preparing for writing

Structure

Stories can follow this pattern:

> **First paragraph**
> Set the scene by giving some details about the main character(s) and saying where and when the story takes place.
>
> (**Note:** You may need to begin your story with the words given.)
>
> **Middle paragraphs**
> Describe what happens.
>
> **Final paragraph**
> Bring the story to a definite conclusion.
>
> (**Note:** You may need to end your story with the words given.)

Selecting information

1 Here are some facts about the story. Some of the words are missing. Fill each gap with one appropriate word.

a Jonathan was a computer p_rogrammer_.
b He carried a black, leather b_riefcase_.
c The two men looked l_ike_ gangsters.
d The tall man carried a case just l_ike_ Jonathan's.
e They both put their cases down at the traffic-l_ights_.
f Jonathan picked up the man's case by m_istake_.
g As the men walked back to their car, they were not yet a_ware_ that anything was wrong.
h He picked up the sales rep's case i_nstead_ of his own.
i The sales company was doing a special o_ffer_ on plastic spiders the next month.
j When the sales rep realized Jonathan had taken her case, she ran a_fter_ him.
k The men caught up w_ith_ Jonathan eventually.
l The tall man a_sked_ Jonathan for his case.
m Jonathan said he only had s_andwiches_ in his case.
n He opened his case and took o_ut_ a gun.
o He p_ointed_ the gun at the men.
p The men ran a_way_.
q The sales rep appeared and took the gun f_rom_ Jonathan.
r It was a water-p_istol_.
s She ha_nded_ Jonathan his case and asked for hers.
t Jonathan went i_nto_ the gardens opposite his office to eat his lunch.
u He opened his case to t_ake_ out his sandwiches.
v He f_ound_ a lot of money in the case instead.
w He c_losed_ the case quickly.

WRITING A STORY   27

2 In **Writing** on page 31 you are going to write a story which begins with these words:

Jonathan left home at the usual time that morning.

Read through your completed sentences on page 27 and decide which information you will probably include in your story. Write these letters in the boxes at the end of the sentences:

E (essential information)
I (interesting but not essential)
X (neither interesting nor essential)

Compare ideas with a partner.

3 Write your final selection in note form in the space provided below.
Remember: You will not be able to include everything that happened when you write out the story. There is a limit of **180** words.

Connecting ideas

1 Time clauses

It is important to include in your story words and phrases which show the time relationship between the events that you describe. Make single sentences from these pairs of sentences. Join the ideas together with *when*, *while*, *as soon as* and *immediately*. Use each one twice.

Example: Jonathan left the house that morning. It was overcast.

When Jonathan left the house that morning, it was overcast.

a The men were waiting to cross the road. Their mobile phone rang.

b The light changed to green. Jonathan crossed the road.

c The men realized what had happened. They set off after Jonathan.

WRITING A STORY

d Jonathan left the newsagent's. He took the sales rep's case instead of his own.

When Jonathan left the newsagent's, he took the sale rep's case instead of his own.

e The sales rep picked up the case. She realized it wasn't hers.

When the sales rep picked up the case, she realized it wasn't hers.

f The men were going up an escalator. Jonathan was walking down the stairs.

When the men were going up an escalator, Jonathan was walking down the stairs.

g Jonathan sat down. He opened his case.

When Jonathan sat down, he opened his case.

h Jonathan saw the money. He couldn't believe his eyes.

When Jonathan saw the money, he couldn't believe his eyes.

2 Participle clauses

We can use an *-ing* clause when two short, connected events are close in time. (**Note:** The subject must be the same in both parts.)

Example: Jonathan picked up the man's case by mistake and crossed the road.

Picking up the man's case by mistake, Jonathan crossed the road.

Rewrite the following sentences as in the example above.

a The tall man opened the case and found Jonathan's sandwiches inside.

Opening the case, the tall man found Jonathan's sandwiches inside.

b The men reversed the car and sped off after Jonathan.

....

c The men got out of the car and followed on foot.

....

d Jonathan protested that his case only contained sandwiches and opened it to show the men.

....

e Jonathan took out the gun and pointed it at the men.

....

f The sales rep took the gun from Jonathan and pulled the trigger.

....

g The sales rep handed Jonathan his case and asked for her own.

....

h Jonathan looked round to check whether anyone had seen him and closed the case.

....

WRITING A STORY   29

Making writing interesting

1 Adverbs

You can make your writing more interesting by adding some descriptive details. One way to do this is to include some adverbs of manner. These give more information about how something is done.

Example: He opened the parcel <u>carefully</u>.

1 Read this sentence and answer the questions which follow.

She packed her bags.

In which 3 places can you put the adverb *quickly* in this sentence?

How does the position of the adverb in the sentence affect its meaning?

2 Fill the gaps in these sentences with the most appropriate adverb from the list below. Use each one once only. In which other places can you put the adverbs?

> frantically   impatiently   menacingly   quickly
> unknowingly   worriedly

a Jonathan waited .... for the lights to change.
b Jonathan .... picked up the wrong case.
c ...., the short man reversed.
d Jonathan .... waved the gun at the two men.
e Jonathan .... looked round to see whether anyone had seen.
f .... Jonathan closed the case.

3 Which adverbs in the previous exercise can the following adverbs replace without changing the meaning of the sentence?

anxiously ....   hastily ....
threateningly ....   unconsciously ....

2 Synonyms

Read these definitions of the verbs *chase*, *pursue* and *follow* below. Then fill the gaps with the best verb in an appropriate form.

> **pursue:** to follow somebody especially in order to catch them (*formal*).
> **chase (after):** to run after somebody in order to catch them (*informal*).
> **follow:** to go after someone to see where they are going and possibly to catch them.

a The woman didn't believe her husband and paid a private detective .... him.
b The singer Madonna .... by photographers wherever she goes.
c My dog likes .... rabbits.
d After .... the escaped prisoner for three days the guards finally caught him.
e Andi's dog .... him everywhere.
f I .... the thief but I didn't manage to catch him.

WRITING A STORY

Writing

Write a **story** of between **120 and 180** words which begins with these words:

Jonathan left home at the usual time that morning.

Choose alternative A or B and follow the **Guidelines** below.

A Retell the original story of *A case of mistaken identity*. Use the notes you made in **Preparing for writing**, Selecting information, on page 27 as the basis of your story.

B Write another story in which the elements of the story are basically the same but the order of events is reversed and one or two details are different.

Use these notes to give you some ideas.

a The tall man's case contains a real gun not money.

b Jonathan goes into the newsagent's first and picks up the sales rep's case. She realizes and chases after Jonathan.

c Jonathan picks up the man's case at the traffic-lights. The men don't realize and attempt to rob a bank with the water pistol. They are caught and blame each other. (Possible end to story)

d The sales rep catches Jonathan, and they exchange cases. Jonathan has his sandwiches back and later eats them unaware of all the problems he has caused. (Possible end to story)

Extra practice

1 Write a **story** of between **120 and 180** words, beginning with these words:

> When Marilyn arrived home, she found the door open.

2 Write a **story** of between **120 and 180** words, ending with these words:

> From that day on he was never the same again.

Guidelines

✓ Do

- Read the instructions carefully. You will have to begin or end your story with the words given.
- Spend a few minutes noting down your ideas in answer to these questions: *Who? When? Where? What happened?*
- Make more detailed notes for each paragraph of your story.
- Write out your story connecting your ideas in different ways and adding detail to make your story more interesting.
- Check grammar, style, spelling and punctuation.

✗ Don't

- Don't start until you are sure what you have to do.
- Don't start writing your story immediately; the thinking and planning stages are important.
- Don't write complete sentences yet. You may decide not to use all your ideas.
- Don't try to include too many events. It is better to describe fewer things in more detail.

WRITING A REPORT Paper 2, Part 2

The Silver Screen

In Part 2 of the Writing paper of the First Certificate in English (FCE) examination, one of the choices may be to write a **report**. A report is a factual piece of writing often based on research. It is usually written in a formal and impersonal style and should have a clear layout with a title and sub-headings.

The examination question will tell you what the topic of the report is, and who the report is for.

Example:

> There is a proposal to open a new multiplex cinema in your neighbourhood. You have been asked to write a short report for the local council on the cinema-going habits of people of your own age-group and say how popular this new cinema would be with them.
>
> Write your **report**.

Think ahead

Questionnaire

Ask your partner these questions and write down their answers.

1. How often do you go to the cinema?
   - once or twice a year
   - once or twice a month
   - two or three times a week
   - once a week
   - other (please specify) _____

2. Where would you place going to the cinema in a list of your favourite activities?
   - 1st
   - 2nd
   - 3rd
   - other (please specify) _____

3. Who do you usually go to the cinema with?
   - friend(s)
   - a boyfriend or girlfriend
   - husband/wife
   - brother or sister
   - parent(s)
   - no one

4. Which day or days do you prefer to go to the cinema?
   - Sun
   - Mon
   - Tues
   - Wed
   - Thurs
   - Fri
   - Sat

5. Which performance do you prefer to go to?
   - Afternoon matinée
   - Evening
   - Late show

6. What are your favourite types of film?
   - action films
   - romantic comedies
   - comedies
   - classics
   - westerns
   - thrillers
   - animated films
   - horror films
   - dramas
   - musicals
   - martial arts films

Discussion

Do you think going to the cinema is better than watching a video at home? What are the advantages of each? Make a note of your ideas. You will need these later.

Cinema:

....

Video:

....

Viewing

Section 1
0.00 - 1.49

In the first section of the video the presenter gives a brief introduction to the cinema, and interviews some people about their cinema-going habits.

Before you watch

Before you watch, try to answer these questions.

1 When was the golden age of the cinema?

   The 1930s ☐   The 1950s ☐

   The 1940s ☐   The 1980s ☐

2 In which decade did fewest people go to the cinema?

   The 1960s ☐   The 1980s ☐

   The 1970s ☐   The 1990s ☐

While you watch

1 Watch this section of the video and check your answers to the questions in **Before you watch**.

2 Write in the answers the people interviewed gave to these questions.

	a How often do you go to the cinema?	b Who do you go with?

WRITING A REPORT   33

Section 2
1.50–3.44

Before you watch

You are going to watch part of an interview with Ralf Ludermann of *Screen International* in which he talks about the film industry. Before you watch, discuss these questions.

1 Why do you think cinema audiences declined in the 1980s?

....

....

2 What advantages do modern multiplex cinemas have over the older single-screen cinemas?

....

....

3 Which 1990s' blockbuster movie attracted people back to the cinema? Why did many of these people become regular cinema-goers again?

....

....

4 Why do so many people go to the cinema nowadays?

....

....

While you watch

1 As you watch this section for the first time, see how many of your ideas above are mentioned.

2 Watch the section again and make a note below of any new ideas you hear. You may find these useful for the writing section later.

a Why did cinema audiences decline in the 1980s?

....

....

b Why was the arrival of the multiplex cinema important in encouraging people to return to the cinema?

....

....

c How did 1990s' blockbusters help the cinema industry?

....

....

d What is the appeal of the cinema to modern audiences?

....

....

34   WRITING A REPORT

Section 3

3.45-4.14

Before you watch

You are going to hear some people explaining why they prefer to go to the cinema than watch a video at home. Before you watch, look back at your ideas in **Discussion** on page 33.

While you watch

1 As you watch this section for the first time, tick (✓) any of your ideas which are mentioned.

2 Watch the section again and note down any different reasons you hear.

....

....

Section 4

4.15-6.27

Before you watch

Before you watch this section, do these exercises.

1 Decide if this information is true (**T**) or false (**F**). Mark the boxes.

   a 26-30 year-olds go to the cinema more often than any other age group. ☐

   b 14-25 year-olds go to the cinema three times a month on average. ☐

   c The most expensive films are often the most successful. ☐

2 Match these actors with their photos. Can you name any of their films?

   Robert de Niro   Kevin Costner   Emma Thompson   Jim Carrey

3 Who are your favourite actors? Make a list.

....

....

While you watch

1 Watch this section and check your answers to **Before you watch 1**. Correct any wrong answers.

2 Listen to these people being interviewed about their favourite types of film. Put a tick (✓) each time you hear one mentioned.

action films	☐	romantic comedies	☐
animated films	☐	thrillers	☐
art films	☐	westerns	☐
classics	☐		
comedies	☐		
dramas	☐		
horror films	☐		
martial arts films	☐		
musicals	☐		

WRITING A REPORT   35

Section 5
6.28–8.18

Before you watch

1 These are the five most successful films of all time to date but they are not in the correct order. Order them from 1 (*the most successful*) to 5.

E.T. ☐   Jurassic Park ☐   Ghost ☐   Star Wars ☐   The Lion King ☐

2 Predict Ralf Ludermann's answer to this question and the reasons he gives.

Do you think that cinema attendance will ever again reach the level it was at in the 1940s?

....

While you watch

1 Watch this section of the video and check your ideas to **Before you watch 1**. Can you add any new titles to the list?

2 Check your answer to **Before you watch 2**. Make a note of any different ideas given.

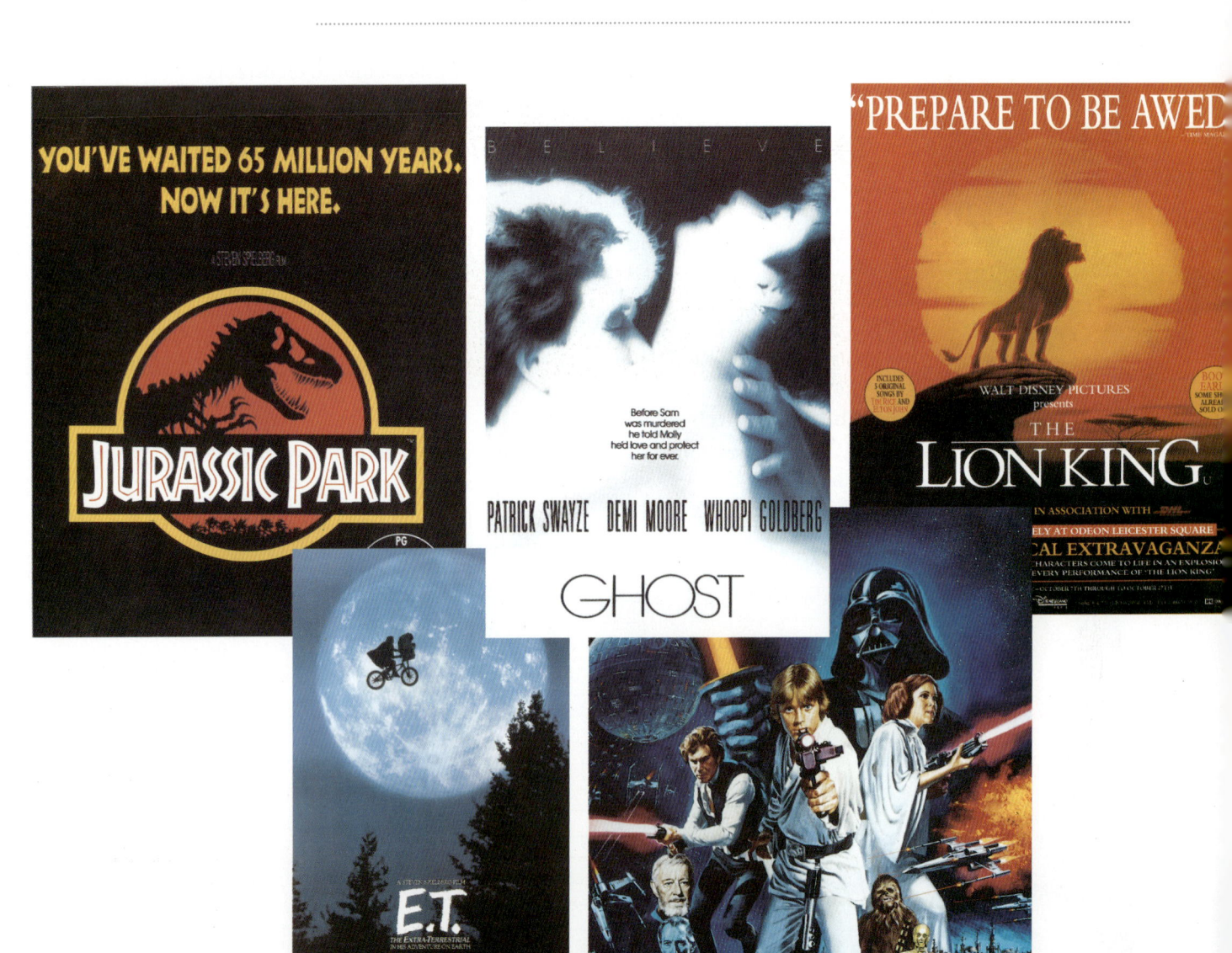

....

36   WRITING A REPORT

Preparing for writing

Structure

Reports can follow this pattern:

> **Title**
> This should be informative:
> - it should tell the reader exactly what the report is about;
> - it should be written in an impersonal, formal style.
>
> **First section**
> This should say what the aim of the report is and, if it is based on a survey, how many people were involved, their ages, socio-economic status, etc.
>
> **Middle sections**
> Each section should deal with one particular aspect of the subject.
>
> **Final section**
> This should summarize the findings. It may include the writer's recommendations but these must be expressed briefly and in an impersonal style.
>
> (**Note:** Each section should have an appropriate sub-heading, which should be brief but informative and written in an impersonal, formal style.)

1 Title

Read these possible titles for the report on page 32. Decide which title or titles are appropriate and which are inappropriate. Give reasons.

a A report on the attitudes and preferences of young people with respect to the cinema

b The golden age of the cinema

c Young people and entertainment

d Young people and the cinema

e The cinema-going habits of young people in (name of town/city)

2 Sub-headings

1 Read the following sub-headings for the report and decide which five are appropriate. Say why the others are inappropriate.

a How often do young people go to the cinema?

b Conclusion

c Attendance patterns

d The kind of films young people like

e Introduction

f People's attitudes to the proposed new multiplex cinema

g The future proposal

h Film preferences

WRITING A REPORT 37

2 Decide on an appropriate order for the five sub-headings you have chosen and say briefly what information you would include under each heading. Think about the questions that were asked in the survey.

....

....

....

Style

Some of the language in the following extracts is inappropriate for a report. Improve the extracts by:

- replacing subjective and informal language with impersonal and formal forms;
- crossing out any unnecessary information;
- making any other necessary changes.

Example:

~~I'm writing~~ *The aim of* this report to ~~tell you about~~ *is summarize* the results of a survey. ~~I did~~ into the cinema-going habits of ~~people my age~~ *young people* in ~~my town~~ *(name of town)*.

a I have based the report on a sample of 200 young people.

These people are 14-24 years old.

b Most of the people that I questioned told me that they went

to the cinema once a week.

c Just about everyone I asked said they liked to go to the evening performance best.

d I asked people if they would go to a multiplex cinema if

they opened one and 25% said 'Yes, if there's free parking!'

e To sum up, it seems clear to me that a multiplex cinema

would be popular and lots of young people in this area would go to it.

Language

1 Expressing numbers

If the report is based on a survey it should include references to numbers.

1 Underline the number language in the following sentences.

a More than half said that they liked comedies.

b Over 150 people said that they went to the cinema at least once a week.

c Up to 10 films can be shown at a time.

d A total of 200 young people were interviewed.

e About 70% said they also liked romantic comedies.

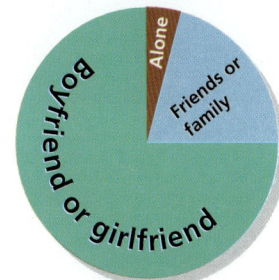

f A large majority (about 80%) said they preferred action films.

g Just under half said that they used public transport to get to the cinema.

h A very small number never went to the cinema.

i Almost 90% said they preferred multiplex cinemas.

j Only a few people never went to the cinema.

2 Using the information given in the pie-charts, write a short paragraph on young people's cinema-going habits and preferences. Try to use as many different number expressions as possible.

2 Expressing opinions

1 Writers can give their opinions in reports but they must express them briefly and in an impersonal style. The following words and phrases are often used to introduce a writer's opinion. Complete them in an appropriate way.

Example: It is surprising that ... *action films are equally popular with young men and women.*

a As might be expected, ...

b It is surprising that ....

c It is interesting that ....

d Not surprisingly, ...

e Strangely, ...

2 Do you know any other words and expressions to replace these?

3 Reporting verbs

Writers often include in their reports some of the questions and answers from the survey. These are almost always written in a reported form.

Choose an appropriate verb from the list below and complete the sentences in a formal and impersonal style. Be brief!

    dislike   disagree   prefer   reply   think

a *I think that cinemas today are much more comfortable than they used to be.*

Several people ....

b *I'd much rather watch a film at the cinema than on video.*

Would you? I wouldn't!

Most people ....

A small percentage ....

c *I can't stand having to watch all the trailers!*

A small minority ....

d Q: *Who do you usually go to the cinema with?*

A: *My boyfriend mostly.*   A: *I usually go with my girlfriend.*

When asked who ....

90% ....

WRITING A REPORT   39

Writing

Write a **report** of between **120 and 180** words in answer to the question on page 32. Read the **Guidelines** below before you start.

Extra practice

Write a **report** of between **120 and 180** words. Choose one of these situations:

1. Your school has decided to provide some money for an after-school activity. The head teacher is considering three possibilities: a cinema club, a keep-fit club or an English club. She has asked you to do a survey on the pupils' preferences and report back to her.

2. The company you work for wants to send some employees on an English course at a language school in Britain. You have found what you think is a suitable school. Write a report for the Head of Training outlining the advantages of sending them there.

Guidelines

✓ Do

- Read the question carefully so that you know exactly what you have to do.
- Decide what type of information your report should contain. If it is based on a survey, write down 4 or 5 questions you would ask.
- Choose an informative title.
- Think of appropriate sub-headings for each section and make notes under these.
- Expand your notes into sentences. Remember to write in a formal and impersonal style. If your report is based on the results of a survey, use number language.
- Read your report through. Check spelling, grammar, punctuation and style.

✗ Don't

- Don't start writing immediately. The thinking and planning stages are important too.
- Don't try to include too much information and don't include irrelevant facts.
- Don't forget to think of a title. An appropriate title will help you get a better mark.
- Don't write long, complicated sub-headings. They should be as brief as possible.
- Don't express strong personal opinions. Comment on facts briefly and impersonally.

WRITING A REPORT

WRITING A LETTER OF APPLICATION   Paper 2, Part 2

Yours Faithfully

In Part 2 of the Writing paper of the First Certificate in English (FCE) examination one of the choices may be to write a **letter of application**. Letters of application are often in reply to an advertisement and may for example take the form of a job application or an application for a grant for further study.

Letters of application should follow a standard layout, be written in formal English and have an appropriate beginning and ending.

The examination question will tell you what you are applying for and who you are writing to.

Example:

You see this advertisement on your college notice board. Write a letter of application saying why you think you are the best person for the job.

Write your **letter** of application.

> **Wanted: Student of English**
> Are you interested in helping to set up an English magazine for other students of English in the college?
> We are looking for someone who meets these requirements:
> • Good at English • Creative • Enjoys writing
> • Works well with others • Hard-working
> Age is not important and experience is not essential.
> If you are interested, send your application to:
> *Joseph Davis, English Department, Room 205A*

Think ahead

Discussion

1 What do you look for in a job? Rank these factors in order of importance from 1-8.

   a Friendly colleagues   e Promotion prospects
   b Pleasant working environment   f Hours of work
   c Good salary   g Long holidays
   d Company pension scheme   h Flexible working hours

2 Compare ideas with a partner. Are there any other important factors you would add to this list?

Role-play

You and your partner are looking for a holiday job. You would like to work together.

Read these advertisements and together decide which job you are most interested in applying for. Do you meet the job requirements?

TEACHERS OF ENGLISH

Teachers of English required for children aged 7-10 on our summer programme (June/July). No experience necessary but you must:
- speak good English
- be 16 or over
- be patient and friendly
- be good with children.

Apply in writing to
Childspeak, Box 2000 Norwich

Fruit pickers

Fruit pickers wanted (June - September): raspberries, strawberries, apples. No experience required. Free accommodation provided. Sundays free. Minimum wage guaranteed.

We are looking for people who are fit, hard-working and reliable.

Apply to:
Hill Farm, Hill Road Cambridge

Holiday camp helpers

Helpers needed at our holiday camps on the Belgian coast to help organize and run the sports/activities programme for 10-14 year-olds.

You must:
★ Be 18 or over
★ Be available to work July-August
★ Like children
★ Speak English
★ Be organized, reliable and enthusiastic
★ Enjoy sports

Apply in writing to
Eurocamp, Box 130, Brussels

Viewing

Section 1
0.00 - 2.44

In the first section of the video you are introduced to the two main characters in the story, Fran and Jeff.

Before you watch

Before you watch this section of the video, predict the answers to the questions below. Use the photos and your imagination to help you.

1 Who are Fran and Jeff? What is their relationship?

2 What is the situation? Why do they look annoyed and fed up?

While you watch

1 Watch the first section and check your ideas to the two questions in **Before you watch**. How different were they from your ideas?

2 Watch this section again. Tick (✓) the job requirements which Fran has and make a note of any details that she gives.

TOUR GUIDES

Magical History Tours requires tour guides for the summer season. Our tours attract many visitors from abroad so you must be able to speak at least one foreign language. You should have an outgoing personality and be able to show leadership qualities.

The jobs will be based in York and candidates will need to be available from June to September.

You must also:
- have an interest in local history
- be good with people
- be enthusiastic and willing to take responsibility
- be at least 18 years of age

Please send your application to:
*The Managing Director,
Magical History Tours,
South Street,
York, YO1 7PD*

MAGICAL
HISTORY TOURS

Dates take her to the start of term ✓

---

3 Answer these questions:

a Why doesn't Jeff want Fran to apply for the job?

....

b What compromise do Jeff and Fran reach?

....

Section 2
2.45-6.17

In this section you will see Fran writing her letter of application, and the managing director and personnel manager deciding which applicants to call for interview.

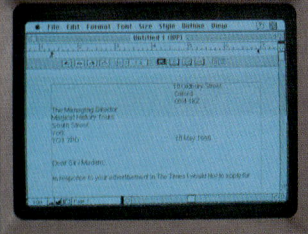

WRITING A LETTER OF APPLICATION   43

Before you watch

1 Predict how Fran will complete the first sentence of her letter of application.

   In response to your advertisement in The Times I ...

2 Discuss how you think the managing director and personnel manager will decide who to call for interview. Make a list of the points you think they will focus on.

   Neatly presented C.V. (word processed, typed or handwritten)

While you watch

1 Watch this section and check your answers to the predictions you made in **Before you watch 2**.

2 The managing director and personnel manager summarize what is good or bad about some of the letters of application.

   Which of the four letters do these sentences relate to? Write 1-4 in the boxes.

   3 • Meets one of the requirements but not another. Sounds ambitious. ☐ 3
   4 • Correct age and an interest in local history. ☐ 4
   1 • Inappropriate style and beginning. ☐ 1
   2 • Inappropriate reason given for wanting the job. ☐ 2

Preparing for writing

Structure

Letters of application may follow this pattern:

Address and date

Write your address without your name in the top right-hand corner. The date goes under this. Write the name and address of the person you are writing to on the left side below the line the date is on. If you don't know the name of the person, write their position.

(**Note:** In the First Certificate Examination you should not write any addresses.)

Beginning a letter

Start with *Dear Sir or Madam* if you do not know the name of the person you are writing to. Start with *Dear Mr/Mrs/Ms(Smith)*, etc. if you know the person by name. Write a comma (,) after the salutation.

First paragraph

In the first paragraph say why you are writing. If you are replying to an advertisement, say where and when you saw it.

> **Middle paragraphs**
>
> Divide your information into paragraphs. List your qualifications and describe your experience giving any relevant details.
>
> Indicate your paragraphs clearly. Either leave a space under the last line of a paragraph or indent the first line of a new paragraph.
>
> **Ending**
>
> Finish your letter with an appropriate concluding remark, for example: *I hope you will consider my application* and add an appropriate ending.
>
> - End 'Dear Sir or Madam' letters *Yours faithfully*.
> - End 'Dear Mr/Mrs/Ms (Smith)' letters *Yours sincerely*.
>
> Finally, sign the letter with your signature. Below this, print your name clearly.

1 Layout

1 Read this successful letter of application. Decide where each section should go on the layout plan. Then say what makes this a good letter of application. Think particularly about register and content.

a *Dear Sir or Madam,*

b *I am seventeen years old but I am considered mature for my age. At present I am studying for my 'A' levels in Economics, Politics and History. In my spare time, I study French and Spanish at evening classes as it is my ambition to work for the UN.*

c *HELEN PROWSE*

d *I lived in York for five years and have always been very interested in the city's history. When I was at school there, I won a prize for my project on York in the Middle Ages.*

e *The Managing Director*
Magical History Tours
South Street
York
YO1 7PD

f *Yours faithfully,*

g *At school I have held a number of positions of responsibility. I am a committee member of our school's history society. I am also the chairperson of our school's debating society and I have organized visits by a number of speakers.*

h *11 May, 1997*

i *109 Telegraph Hill*
Liverpool
L75 5WI

j *H Prowse*

k *I hope that you will consider my application. I look forward to hearing from you.*

l *I have just seen your advertisement in The Times for tour guides, and I would like to apply.*

WRITING A LETTER OF APPLICATION

2 Read this unsuccessful letter of application. Say what is wrong with it. Think about layout, register and content.

> Andrea Cousins
> 17 Causeway Drive
> Bath
> BA10 1JP
>
> Dear Sir
> I want to apply for the job of tour guide. I'm 19 and I'm quite interested in local history. I haven't been to York before so I don't know a lot about it but I'm keen to learn. I worked as a tour guide for a month in Bath last summer so I've got some experience of working as a guide. I liked it a lot. I'm a responsible person and I'm good with people.
>
> I hope you write back soon.
>
> Yours sincerely
> *A Cousins*

The sender's name is not written before the sender's address

2 Opening paragraphs

In your opening paragraph you should say why you are writing and where (and when) you saw the job advertisement.

Complete these opening paragraphs in an appropriate way after first putting the words in the correct order. Write the complete sentence in the space provided.

a guides advertisement to your reply in tour for ...

In reply to your advertisement for tour guide I'very would like to reply to your

b apply job would tour as I like the guide for to of ...

I would like to apply for the job of tour guide as

c writing your regard am with I to ...

I'm writing with regard to your

d yesterday's reference with advertisement to edition in your ...

With reference to your advertisement in yesterday's edition

reply — responder

regard — considerar

reference — referencia

46 WRITING A LETTER OF APPLICATION

Connecting ideas

The words *and, but, so, because* and *although* are frequently used to combine parts of sentences. Complete the sentences below using your own ideas.

a I speak fluent German **and** my ....

b I have never worked as a tour guide before **but** ....

c My mother comes from France **so** ....

d I organized a tour to Canterbury **and** ....

e I speak fluent French **because** ....

f **Although** I do not know York very well, ...

g I have no previous experience as a guide **but** ....

h I did a project on the development of the city of York last year **so** ....

i **Although** I am only seventeen, ...

j I think I would make a good tour guide **because** ....

Vocabulary

Match the sentence beginnings with the best endings and join them with an appropriate preposition from the list below.

| for | in | of | to | with |

a I am interested — *in* — the history of the city of York.
b I am capable — *of* — being with foreigners.
c I would be pleased — *to* — applying for the job of tour guide.
d I have been involved — *in* — interview any afternoon.
e I am familiar — *with* — come for an interview at your convenience.
f I would be available — *to* — organizing a trip to Canterbury.
g When I was at school, I was responsible — *for* — taking responsibility.
h I am accustomed — *to* — work long hours if necessary.
i I would be willing — *to* — running several clubs.

b.) I'm capable of taking responsibility.
c.) I would be pleased to come for an interview ...
d.) I have been involved with organizing
e.) I'm familiar with the history of N.Y.

WRITING A LETTER OF APPLICATION

Writing

Read the advertisement for the job of tour guide on page 43 and write Fran's **letter of application** of between **120 and 180** words. Follow the **Guidelines** below and use your imagination as well as the information you already have. Remember to give examples to support your application.

(**Note:** Fran's full name is *Francesca Lawson*.)

Extra practice

Read the advertisement for the job on page 41. Write a **letter of application** of between **120 and 180** words for this job.

Guidelines

✓ Do

- Read the instructions carefully and make sure you know what to do.
- Make notes for each paragraph. Give relevant details about yourself and remember to support these with examples.
- Begin your letter in an appropriate way. Use the person's name, if you know it, *Dear (Mr White)*. If not, write *Dear Sir or Madam*.
- Expand your notes into sentences. Remember to write in formal English and join your ideas with appropriate linkers.
- End your letter in an appropriate way. Remember to sign your name in full and print it under your signature.
- Check grammar, spelling, punctuation and register.

✗ Don't

- Don't start to write immediately. The thinking and planning stages are very important.
- Don't write complete sentences yet.
- Don't include any addresses or the date. It isn't necessary for the First Certificate examination.
- Don't use contractions or any idiomatic expressions.
- Don't add a *P.S.* even if you have forgotten to say something.

WRITING A LETTER OF APPLICATION

WRITING A DISCURSIVE COMPOSITION Paper 2, Part 2

The Dream Machine

In Part 2 of the Writing paper of the First Certificate in English (FCE) examination, one of the choices may be to write a **discursive composition**.

There are two common forms of this type of composition. You may be asked to consider, in a balanced way, the advantages and disadvantages of a particular idea, institution or object.

Example:

> What are the advantages and disadvantages of travelling by car?

or to give your personal opinion about a given subject.

Example:

> Within the next few years, driving a car will become a socially unacceptable activity. Do you agree?

Think ahead

Discussion

1 Which of these scenes is most similar to where you live?

2 What are the attractions of owning and driving a car?

Questionnaire

1 Work through this questionnaire.

> 1 Can you drive? YES ☐ NO ☐
>
> 2 How many people in your family can drive? ☐
>
> 3 What kinds of public transport are available in your town or your area?
>   Tick (✓) kinds available. ☐ bus ☐ tram ☐ train ☐ underground
>
> 4 How do you usually travel in these situations? Tick (✓) one option.
>
> | | by public transport | by car | on foot |
> |---|---|---|---|
> | • to get to school, college or work | ☐ | ☐ | ☐ |
> | • to get to your main shopping area | ☐ | ☐ | ☐ |
> | • to go out for the evening (e.g. cinema, disco, club, a party, etc.) | ☐ | ☐ | ☐ |
> | • to visit friends | ☐ | ☐ | ☐ |
> | • to go on holiday | ☐ | ☐ | ☐ |
>
> 5 How often and when do you use taxis?
>   _____
>
> 6 Are there any occasions when you would definitely not use a car?
>   _____
>
> 7 What are your main reasons for not using a car?
>   _____

2 Compare and discuss your answers with other students.

How dependent are you and your family on cars?

Viewing

Section 1
0.00 – 3.50

Before you watch

1 The first section of the video you are going to watch is about the disadvantages of driving and owning a car. Before you watch, predict what disadvantages will be mentioned.

Disadvantages of driving and owning a car

....

....

....

....

2 Compare lists with a partner.

WRITING A DISCURSIVE COMPOSITION

While you watch

1 Watch the first section and check how many of the disadvantages you listed are mentioned, either by the presenter or by the people who are interviewed.

2 In pairs discuss any 'new' disadvantages mentioned by the speakers.

3 Watch the interviews again and match the disadvantages (a-g) mentioned by the speakers with their pictures (1-6). Write the speakers numbers in the spaces alongside the disadvantages. (**Note:** The same disadvantages may be mentioned by more than one speaker.)

Speakers

Disadvantages

a cars use a lot of petrol ....
b selfish behaviour of other drivers ....
c frequent break-downs ....
d traffic jams ....
e owning a car is expensive ....
f cars lose their value very quickly ....
g thefts of car radios and damage caused ....

Section 2

3.51 - 5.48

Before you watch

What are the pros and cons of using public transport? Brainstorm ideas in pairs for 2-3 minutes. Write a list of points here.

Pros: Cons:

WRITING A DISCURSIVE COMPOSITION   51

While you watch

You are going to hear people talking about their dependence on their cars, and their attitudes to public transport.

1 Watch and tick any of the points mentioned that you noted on page 51.

2 Watch again and complete this table with short answers. If the speakers don't answer a question, put a cross (✗). (**Note:** Some sample answers are included.)

a Could he or she survive without a car?	No					
b Where does he or she live?						
c When or for what reasons does he or she use his/her car?				job		
d What other form(s) of transport does he or she use?	✗				none	

Section 3

5.49 – 8.16

Before you watch

1 The presenter is going to ask five people this question:

Are you at all concerned about the environment when you use your car?

What does the word 'environment' mean in this context?

2 Here are some possible answers to this question. Predict which one of these answers the five people agree with.

a My car has got nothing to do with the environment.

b I am not at all concerned about the environment.

c I am worried about the environment but not enough to stop using my car.

d I feel guilty every time I use my car.

e I hardly ever use my car because of the damage it does to the environment.

3 What answer would you give if you were asked this question?

While you watch

1 Watch the last part of the video and check your predictions.

2 Which speaker do you most agree with?

3 What do you think should be done to make public transport more attractive to car users? Here are some ideas.

- Cost
- Comfort
- Convenience
- Frequency

52 WRITING A DISCURSIVE COMPOSITION

Preparing for writing

Structure

Discursive compositions can follow this pattern:

> **First paragraph**
> An introduction to the subject and an indication of the kind of composition this is going to be.
>
> **Middle paragraphs**
> Here are two common paragraph patterns:
>
> - One or more paragraphs dealing with advantages only, followed by one or more paragraphs dealing with disadvantages only.
>
> - One or more paragraphs dealing with advantages and disadvantages of ONE aspect of the topic, followed by one or more paragraphs dealing with advantages and disadvantages of ANOTHER aspect.
>
> **Last paragraph**
> A summary of the main ideas and a concluding statement, which may include the writer's opinion.

Read through these first, middle and last paragraphs written by students of English. How effective are they?

1 First paragraphs

a Most big cities around the world suffer from traffic problems. The reason for this is the fact that most people like driving their own car.

b In my essay I'm going to discuss the pros and cons of having a car.

c We are living in the late 20th century. If we start talking about modern civilization, we can't forget cars. Imagine deserted cities without cars, taxis and buses. But these faithful vehicles have got bad aspects as well as good ones. Now I'm going to think of the advantages and disadvantages of owning a car.

2 Middle paragraphs (extracts)

a The advantages are you can go anywhere and cars are more comfortable than any other means of transport. In a car you can carry a lot of stuff. Another advantage is you are safe in your car and nobody can hurt you.

b But there are some disadvantages. First of all, cars are very expensive to own and drive. In addition to the price of the car, you have to pay for petrol, insurance and repairs. Also, while you are driving you may get stuck in a traffic jam or have a serious accident.

c In the first place, drivers often say that cars are convenient and it is true that you can go from your home to anywhere else when you want to. On the other hand, roads are often crowded with traffic and it takes you longer to travel than by train. So in this case it is not so convenient.

WRITING A DISCURSIVE COMPOSITION

3 Last paragraphs

a *To sum up, my opinion is that a car can be very useful just as long as we use it for normal distances and do not drive to the shop in the next street. Why don't we all repair our bicycles?*

b *In conclusion, owning a car is a kind of twentieth century luxury that people have to pay for in one way or another.*

c *To conclude, I'll walk as much as I can and I'll enjoy doing so.*

Connecting ideas

It is important to include in your composition words and phrases which help the reader to understand how you have organized your writing. Words and phrases of this kind often appear at the beginnings of paragraphs or sentences.

1 Can you add other words and phrases to the group below? (**Note:** Some of them were introduced in **All you need to know**, Connecting ideas, page 12.)

- to introduce a new topic or idea

    One advantage of cars **is that** they give you freedom.

    one advantage … is that …

    To begin

- to introduce additional information

    As well as giving you freedom, cars **also** make people …

    as well as … also …

    in addicion can give you freedom

- to introduce contrasting information

    On the one hand … / **On the other hand**, private cars …

    on the one hand … on the other hand …

    On the contrary of everbody thinks, you have a lot of problems with cars.

- to introduce summarizing or concluding remarks

    In conclusion, it seems that the car is here to stay.

    in conclusion …

    to conclude, it seems that the probably of cars on the street is getting each day worst

Other words and phrases can be used:

- to make generalizations

    On the whole, people are aware of the problems

    on the whole …

    To my mind

54 WRITING A DISCURSIVE COMPOSITION

- to support generalizations

  In my town, **for example**, ...

  for example ...

  ....

  ....

- to introduce personal opinions

  I believe that cars are fundamentally harmful to ...

  I believe that ...

  ....

  ....

2 Underline any similar words and phrases used in the sample paragraphs in **Structure** on pages 53-54. Which of the above categories do they belong to?

Style

In general, discursive compositions should be written in a formal style.

1 Make a list of features of this kind of writing. Compare lists with a partner.

2 Read these composition extracts. How could they be improved? Underline any inappropriate words or phrases and then rewrite the extracts.

> The best thing about cars is that you can travel from door to door. I mean if you're on a bus you've got to get off at a bus stop and walk to where you're going and that's not very convenient, is it? So it's better if you've got your own car. Then, of course, you don't get so tired if you're in your own car.

> Now I'm going to think about not having a car. Of course, I'll probably save lots of money, because it's expensive to have a car and I'd have to walk everywhere so I'd be really healthy. At the moment I'm pretty unfit because I always drive. And if you're on foot, you don't have to worry about finding a parking space. Last week it took me twenty minutes to find somewhere to park in my town.

3 If you want to include people's words in your composition, you can use direct speech:
Example: *I use my car to go to work.*

It is usually better, however, to use reported speech.
Example:
I asked my eighty-year-old grandfather how many cars there were on the road when he was young compared with now. **He said there were a lot more cars on the roads nowadays. He said that his parents had never had enough money to buy a car.**

How could these extracts from the video interviews be included in a composition? Rewrite them in reported speech.
Example:
I shout all the time. That's quite fun. I like that.
One young woman said she quite enjoyed shouting at other drivers.

a *Well, the worst thing about owning my car, specifically, is that it breaks down a lot because it's so old, and it eats petrol so it costs quite a lot of money.*

b *Once you have a car, it's difficult to imagine living without it because it gives you so much more freedom. If you want to go somewhere, you can go without thinking.*

c *I don't think I could do the job I'm doing without a car; but yes, I could survive without a car.*

Vocabulary

1 Cars and driving

What are the differences in meaning between these pairs of words? Discuss your ideas with a partner, then check your answers with your teacher or by looking in a dictionary.

   a   travel / journey

   b   injury / damage

   c   accident / breakdown

   d   main road / motorway

   e   traffic / vehicle

   f   smoke / fumes

   g   petrol / oil

   h   parking space / car park

2 Verbs and nouns

1   Which verbs in list A commonly go with the nouns in list B?

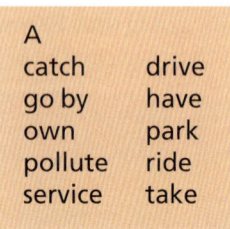

A		B	
catch	drive	accident	air
go by	have	car	city
own	park	atmosphere	bus
pollute	ride	train	taxi
service	take	bicycle	motorbike

2   Make up sentences using some of these verb-noun combinations.

   Example: *I've been driving a car since I was 18.*

3 Compound nouns

Make compound nouns from these phrases.

   a   accidents on motorways

   b   pollution of the air

   c   centres of cities

   d   costs of motoring

   e   queues of traffic

   f   fines for speeding

   g   fumes from car exhausts

   h   a radio in a car

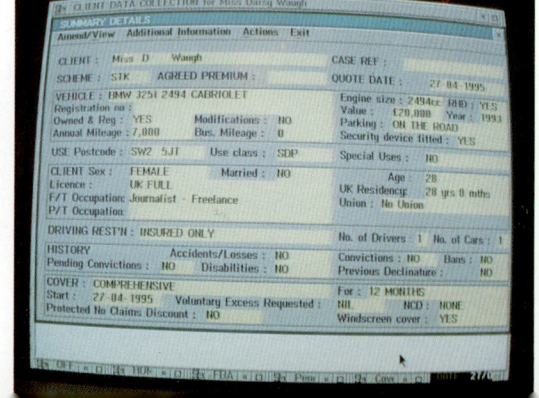

WRITING A DISCURSIVE COMPOSITION

Writing

Write a **composition** of between **120 and 180** words in answer to this question:

What are the advantages and disadvantages of owning a car?

Use your own ideas, in addition to any of the ideas that you have noted down while you were working through the video. Also, read and follow the **Guidelines** below.

Extra practice

Write a **composition** of between **120 and 180** words. Choose one of these topics.

1. What are the advantages and disadvantages of living in a village or small town?

2. By the year 2050 life in big cities will be so dangerous and unhealthy that people will go back to living in country areas. How far do you agree?

Guidelines

✓ Do

- Read the question carefully so that you know exactly what you have to do. What kind of discursive composition is this?
- Make a paragraph plan. Note down two or three advantages and two or three disadvantages you intend to include in the middle paragraphs. Think about how you could summarize your ideas in a concluding paragraph.
- Write your composition, following your paragraph plan and using appropriate connecting words and phrases. Support any generalizations you make with specific examples.
- Write in an appropriately formal style.
- Read through your composition checking spelling, grammar, punctuation and style.

✗ Don't

- Don't start writing immediately. Think and plan first.
- Don't try to include too many different advantages and disadvantages. It is important to select what you think are the most important points.
- Don't leave the reader to guess how you have organized your composition.
- Don't use too much informal language.

WRITING A DISCURSIVE COMPOSITION

SAMPLE QUESTIONS AND ANSWERS

1 Transactional letter

Sample question

You want to spend a holiday in Britain and your English penfriend has sent you a letter, together with an advert for a holiday cottage. You think the cottage sounds interesting but you would like some more information.

Read the advert and your penfriend's letter, together with your own notes. Then write a reply to your penfriend, asking all your questions and giving the information your friend needs.

> Why don't you rent one of these cottages? They're near the sea, and I'm sure you would enjoy Scotland. Let me know what dates you want to come, and I'll find out if there is one available and how much it costs.

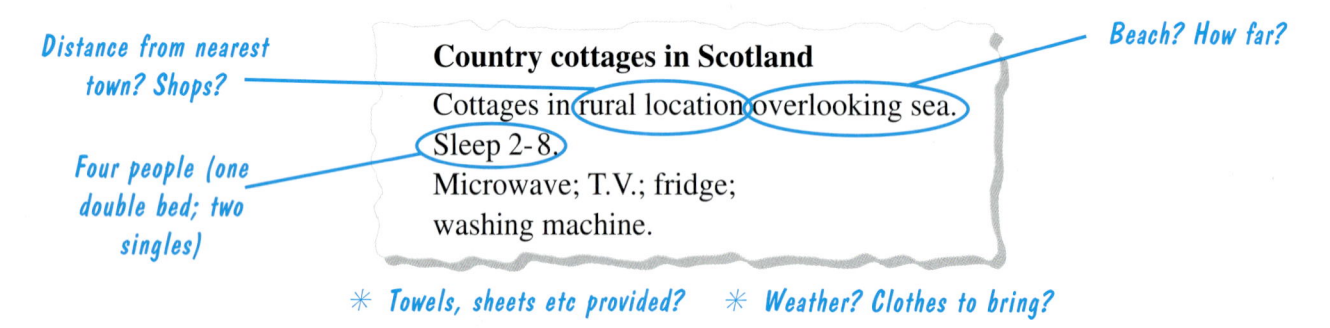

Distance from nearest town? Shops?

Four people (one double bed; two singles)

Country cottages in Scotland
Cottages in rural location overlooking sea.
Sleep 2-8.
Microwave; T.V.; fridge; washing machine.

Beach? How far?

✻ *Towels, sheets etc provided?* ✻ *Weather? Clothes to bring?*

Write a **letter** of between **120 and 180** words in an appropriate style. Do not write any addresses.

Sample answer

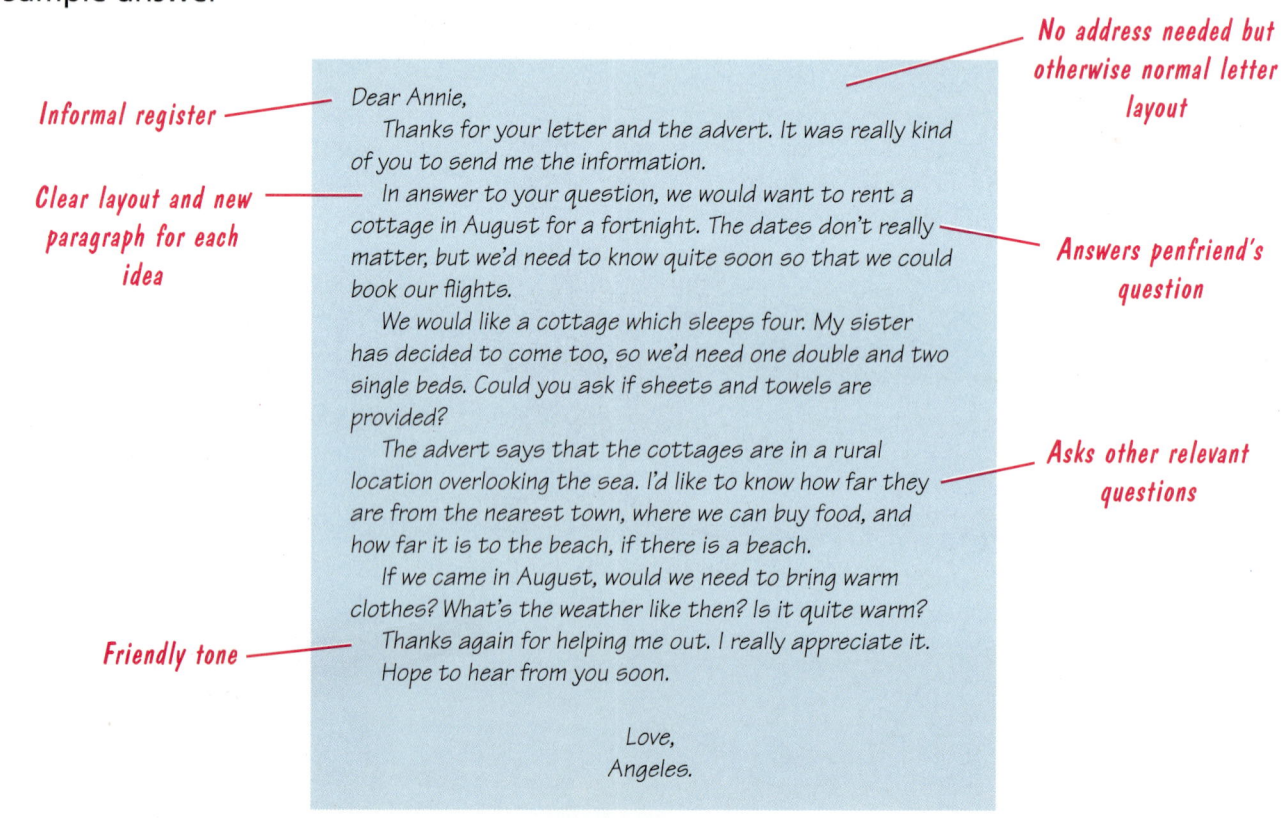

Informal register

Clear layout and new paragraph for each idea

Friendly tone

Dear Annie,
   Thanks for your letter and the advert. It was really kind of you to send me the information.
   In answer to your question, we would want to rent a cottage in August for a fortnight. The dates don't really matter, but we'd need to know quite soon so that we could book our flights.
   We would like a cottage which sleeps four. My sister has decided to come too, so we'd need one double and two single beds. Could you ask if sheets and towels are provided?
   The advert says that the cottages are in a rural location overlooking the sea. I'd like to know how far they are from the nearest town, where we can buy food, and how far it is to the beach, if there is a beach.
   If we came in August, would we need to bring warm clothes? What's the weather like then? Is it quite warm?
   Thanks again for helping me out. I really appreciate it. Hope to hear from you soon.

                                   Love,
                                   Angeles.

No address needed but otherwise normal letter layout

Answers penfriend's question

Asks other relevant questions

2 Article

Sample question

You see this advertisement in an international magazine for young people:

> **Your say**
> What is there for young people to do in your town?
> Write an article giving your views. The writers of all articles published will receive one year's free subscription to the magazine of their choice.

Write an **article** between **120 and 180** words based on your own experience.

Sample answer

Interesting title

Opening sentence which makes us want to read more

New paragraph for each point

Appropriate informal style

Final paragraph, which rounds off the article

> <u>There's nothing to do</u>
>
> If you ask young people in Witham if they like living there, most of them will answer, 'No. It's boring! There's nothing to do!' Is this true, or is this what young people always say no matter where they live?
>
> If you like night-life, it is true that compared with London and other big cities there isn't much to do. There's only one cinema, and although there are several discos, they are only open to people under eighteen on two nights a week. Some of the pubs have live music but you have to be over eighteen to go there, too.
>
> If you like sport, the facilities are quite good. There is a leisure centre, where you can swim, play squash and do other sports, but it's too expensive to use every day.
>
> To be honest, if you're under eighteen there isn't a lot to do. But Witham is no different from towns of a similar size in the rest of the country. To young people they are all equally 'boring'.

3 Story

Sample question

Your teacher has asked you to write a story which begins with these words:

I had never been so frightened in my whole life.

Write a **story** of between **120 and 180** words.

Sample answer

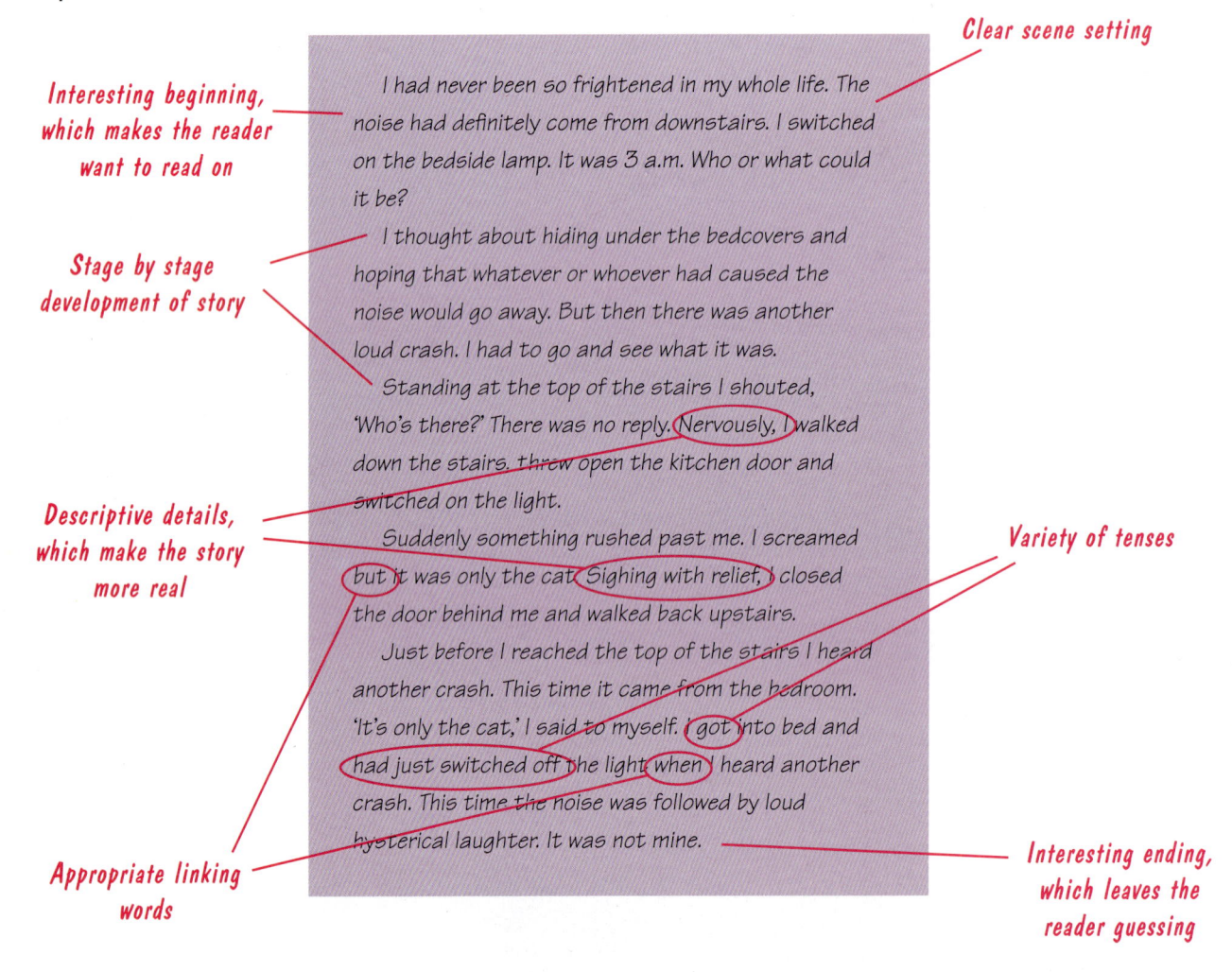

> I had never been so frightened in my whole life. The noise had definitely come from downstairs. I switched on the bedside lamp. It was 3 a.m. Who or what could it be?
>
> I thought about hiding under the bedcovers and hoping that whatever or whoever had caused the noise would go away. But then there was another loud crash. I had to go and see what it was.
>
> Standing at the top of the stairs I shouted, 'Who's there?' There was no reply. Nervously, I walked down the stairs, threw open the kitchen door and switched on the light.
>
> Suddenly something rushed past me. I screamed but it was only the cat. Sighing with relief, I closed the door behind me and walked back upstairs.
>
> Just before I reached the top of the stairs I heard another crash. This time it came from the bedroom. 'It's only the cat,' I said to myself. I got into bed and had just switched off the light when I heard another crash. This time the noise was followed by loud hysterical laughter. It was not mine.

Annotations:
- *Interesting beginning, which makes the reader want to read on*
- *Clear scene setting*
- *Stage by stage development of story*
- *Descriptive details, which make the story more real*
- *Variety of tenses*
- *Appropriate linking words*
- *Interesting ending, which leaves the reader guessing*

SAMPLE QUESTIONS AND ANSWERS

4 Report

Sample question

Your college has asked you to write a report for its international students on a discotheque in your town. Your report should cover:

- Its location and price
- The atmosphere
- The music
- The food and drink served there

Write a **report** of between **120 and 180** words.

Sample answer

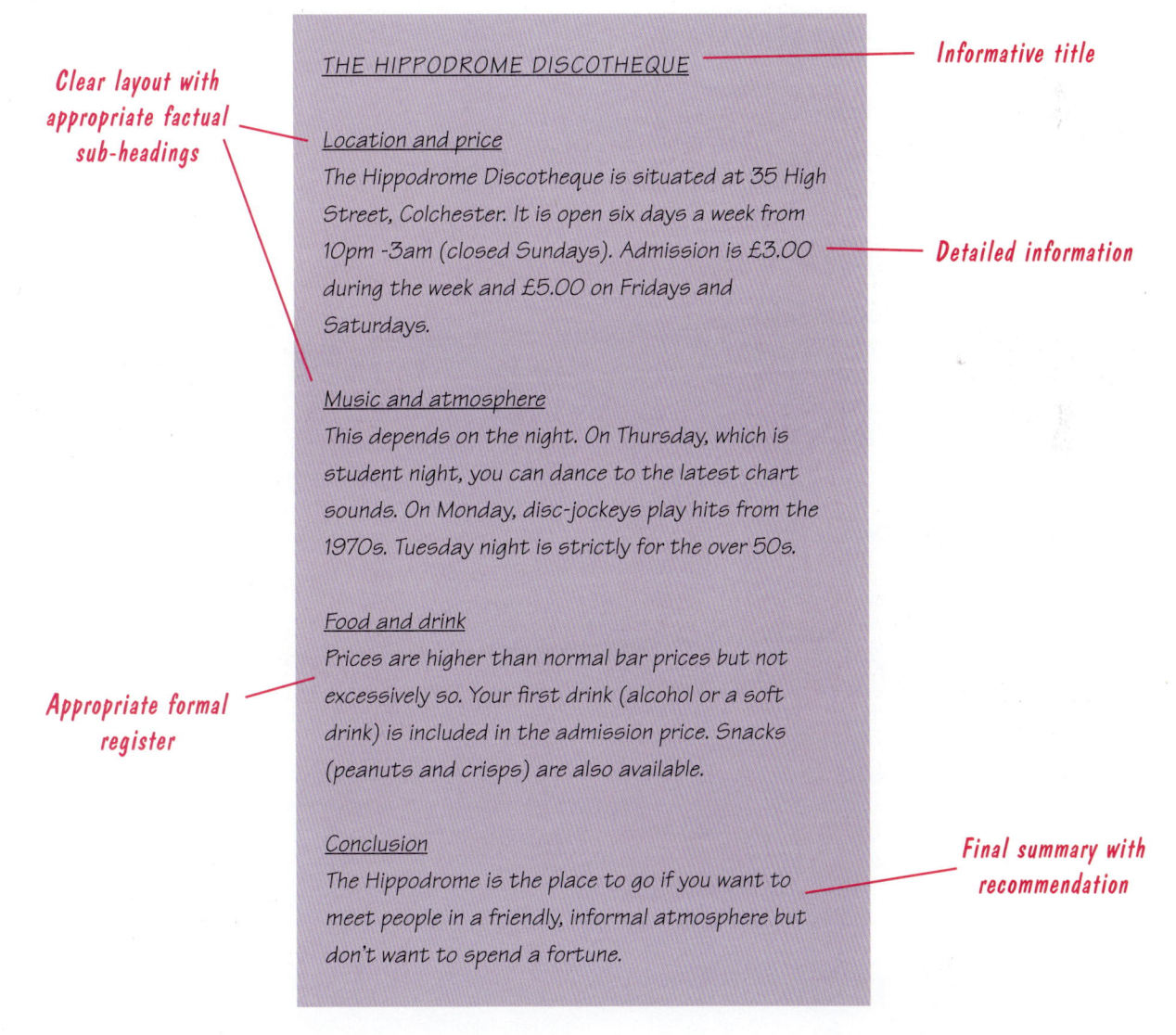

THE HIPPODROME DISCOTHEQUE — *Informative title*

Clear layout with appropriate factual sub-headings

Location and price
The Hippodrome Discotheque is situated at 35 High Street, Colchester. It is open six days a week from 10pm -3am (closed Sundays). Admission is £3.00 during the week and £5.00 on Fridays and Saturdays. — *Detailed information*

Music and atmosphere
This depends on the night. On Thursday, which is student night, you can dance to the latest chart sounds. On Monday, disc-jockeys play hits from the 1970s. Tuesday night is strictly for the over 50s.

Food and drink
Prices are higher than normal bar prices but not excessively so. Your first drink (alcohol or a soft drink) is included in the admission price. Snacks (peanuts and crisps) are also available.

Appropriate formal register

Conclusion
The Hippodrome is the place to go if you want to meet people in a friendly, informal atmosphere but don't want to spend a fortune. — *Final summary with recommendation*

5 Letter of application

Sample question

You have seen this advertisement for a holiday job in a newspaper and want to apply.

E.L. Organization

E.L. Organization runs English language courses for children aged 9-11 in Britain in July and August.

We are looking for helpers who meet the following requirements:
- Sensible and mature
- 18 or over
- Good spoken English
- Reliable

You will :
- accompany the children from your country to Britain and back.
- be responsible for their welfare during the trip and while they are in Britain.

In return you will receive: free transport and accommodation; all meals; free English classes.

Write to:
E.L. Organization, P.O. Box 7180, London.

Write a **letter of application** of between **120 and 180** words, saying why you think you are a suitable person for this job.

Sample answer

Dear Sir or Madam,

    I am writing in reply to your advertisement for helpers in yesterday's Times.

    I am eighteen years old, and I have just left school. I am starting university in the autumn so I would be available to work in July and August.

    I have a good level of spoken English. I passed the Cambridge First Certificate examination last December with a B grade, and I have been to England twice. I would very much like to have the opportunity to go there again and improve my English, which is one of the subjects I will be studying at university.

    I think I am a sensible, mature and reliable person. Last summer I looked after children at a summer camp in France. I was responsible for organizing and supervising all the outdoor activities for the children, who were aged 7-9.

    I hope you will consider my application. I would be happy to send you references from my previous employers if you require them.

Yours faithfully,

EJM Garcia

Eduardo Garcia.

Annotations:
- Formal register
- Clear statement giving reason for writing
- No address needed but otherwise normal letter layout
- Relevant information to support application

SAMPLE QUESTIONS AND ANSWERS

6 Composition

Sample question

Your English teacher has asked all the students in your class to write an answer to this question:

> What are the advantages and disadvantages of old people living with younger members of their families?

Write a **composition** of between **120 and 180** words outlining the advantages and disavantages and giving examples.

Sample answer

These days people are living longer than they used to. Unfortunately, however, many old people cannot look after themselves and have to go and live with their families. Naturally, there are advantages and disadvantages to this situation.

In the first place, if they are ill, old people will be well looked after by their own families. Secondly, people of different generations learn how to live with and understand each other. Also, from a practical point of view, old people themselves can be helpful. For example, they can do babysitting.

On the other hand, there are disadvantages. For instance, some old people like peace and quiet and may find it difficult to live in a family where there are young children. This could lead to arguments and disagreements. In addition to this, many old people do not like to lose their independence.

In conclusion, I think there are many benefits to old people living with their families. As long as everyone is prepared to compromise, it can be a happy and successful experience all round.

Appropriate general statement on topic

Clear layout with advantages and disadvantages in separate paragraphs.

Appropriate connecting phrases

Development of main point with examples

Final summary of arguments

WRITING BANK

Features of formal and informal writing

In the First Certificate examination you need to be able to show that you can produce the two main styles of written English: formal and informal. These lists are a reminder of the main features of each style.
(**Note:** The numbers in brackets refer to the sample answers on pages 58-63)

Formal

- longer sentences
  As long as everyone is prepared to compromise, it can be a happy and successful experience all round. (6)
- impersonal tone
  Naturally, there are advantages and disadvantages to this situation.
- full verb forms
  I have been to England twice. (5)
- polite phrases
  I would be happy to send you references from my previous employers ... (5)
- passive verbs
  Your first drink is included in the admission price. (4)
- single-word verbs
  ... and improve my English ...(informal would be: brush up) (5)
- include pronouns
  I am starting university in the autumn so I would be available ... (5)
- avoidance of slang or colloquial forms
  I would very much like ...(5) *(informal could be : It'd be really great to ...)*

Informal

- shorter sentences
  Thanks for your letter and the advert. (1)
- personal tone
  To be honest, if you're under eighteen there isn't a lot to do. (2)
- shortened verb forms
  ... we'd need one double and two single beds. (1)
- no especially polite phrases
- active verbs
  Some of the pubs have live music ...(2) *(formal could be: Live music is played in some of the pubs.)*
- phrasal verbs
  Thanks again for helping me out. (1)
- sometimes leave out pronouns
  (I) Hope to hear from you soon. (1)
- some slang or colloquial forms included
  The dates don't really matter ...(1)

Connecting words and phrases

Here are some connecting words and phrases you may find useful in any of the writing tasks you have to do in the First Certificate examination. They will help you to organize your writing by linking sentences and paragraphs to each other.

Sequencing events	Introducing contrasting information	Summarizing or concluding	Introducing an opinion	Making generalizations
after	however	in conclusion	as far as I'm concerned	on the whole
as soon as	in contrast	in short	as might be expected	in general
by the time	nevertheless	on balance	I believe (that)	by and large
immediately	on the contrary	on the whole	I feel that	
just before	on the other hand	taking X, Y and Z into	in my opinion	
when	whereas	account	in my view	
while	but	to conclude	interestingly/	
		to sum up	surprisingly/ strangely,	
Introducing additional information	**Introducing an example**	to summarize	etc.	
another advantage ...	for instance	**Introducing new information**	it is interesting/ surprising,	
another point ...	for example	first of all	etc. (that)	
apart from		firstly/secondly, etc.	not surprisingly	
as well as		in the first place	to my mind	
besides		my second point is		
in addition (to)		lastly		
on the one hand		finally		
what is more				